Edexcel A2 Music
Revision Guide

by

Alistair Wightman

RHINEGOLD
EDUCATION

www.rhinegoldeducation.co.uk

Music Study Guides
GCSE, AS and A2 Music Study Guides (AQA, Edexcel and OCR)
GCSE, AS and A2 Music Listening Tests (AQA, Edexcel and OCR)
AS/A2 Music Technology Study Guide (Edexcel)
AS/A2 Music Technology Listening Tests (Edexcel)
Revision Guides for GCSE, AS and A2 (AQA, Edexcel and OCR)

Also available from Rhinegold Education
Key Stage 3 Listening Tests: Book 1 and Book 2
AS and A2 Music Harmony Workbooks
GCSE and AS Music Composition Workbooks
GCSE and AS Music Literacy Workbooks

Baroque Music in Focus, Film Music in Focus, Musicals in Focus
Music Technology from Scratch
Dictionary of Music in Sound
Understanding Popular Music

First published 2011 in Great Britain by
Rhinegold Education
14–15 Berners Street
London W1T 3LJ
www.rhinegoldeducation.co.uk

© 2011 Rhinegold Education
a division of Music Sales Limited

You should always check the current requirements of the examination, since these may change.
Copies of the Edexcel specification can be downloaded from the Edexcel website at www.edexcel.com
Telephone: 01623 467467   Email: publications@linneydirect.com

Edexcel A2 Music Revision Guide
Order No. RHG340
ISBN 978-1-78038-065-0

Exclusive Distributors:
Music Sales Ltd
Distribution Centre, Newmarket Road
Bury St Edmunds, Suffolk IP33 3YB, UK

Printed in the EU

Contents

THE AUTHOR

Alistair Wightman read Music at Oxford and then York University, where he was awarded a D. Phil for his study of the music of Karol Szymanowski. He has worked in primary, secondary and further education, and is a freelance teacher and writer as well as principal examiner in history and analysis in A-level music. His publications include *Writing about Music* (Rhinegold, 2008) and several books and articles devoted to Tadeusz Baird, Karłowicz and Szymanowski, including *Karłowicz, Young Poland and the Musical Fin-de-siècle* (Ashgate, 1996), *Karol Szymanowski: his Life and Music* (Ashgate, 1999) and *Szymanowski on Music: Selected Writings of Karol Szymanowski* (Toccata Press, 1999).

ACKNOWLEDGEMENTS

The author would like to thank the consultant Hugh Benham and the Rhinegold Education editorial and design team of Matthew Hammond, Harriet Power and Christina Forde for their expert support in the preparation of this book.

COPYRIGHT

Introduction

For the Edexcel A2 qualification in Music you have to complete the following parts:

➤ Unit 4: Extended Performance (30% of the total A2 mark)

➤ Unit 5: Composition and Technical Study (30% of the total A2 mark)

➤ Unit 6: Further Musical Understanding (40% of the total A2 mark).

At the start of the summer term, it is quite likely that you will still have to finish Units 4 and 5. Try to complete these assignments as promptly as possible in order to leave more time to revise for the Unit 6 examination.

SET WORKS

This revision guide is designed to help you prepare for Unit 6, an externally-assessed examination that lasts two hours. The paper is divided into three sections, and this guide deals particularly with Sections B (Music in Context) and C (Continuity and Change in Instrumental Music). Some tips are given on pages 7–11 concerning Section A (Aural Analysis), although you will find more coverage on this section, along with test material, in Rhinegold Education's *Edexcel A2 Music Listening Tests* (3rd edition).

The mark total for Unit 6 is 90, distributed as follows:

➤ Section A: 28

➤ Section B: 26

➤ Section C: 36

Unit 6

The set works change annually, so make sure that you study the correct music for the year you are taking the examination. All the prescribed works are taken from *The New Anthology of Music* (*NAM*) edited by Julia Winterson (Edexcel, 2008), and details of the requirements for each year are given below. Bear in mind that, though based on music which may well be unfamiliar to you, Section A (Aural Analysis) questions will focus on genres and styles that you have studied for Sections B and C. Note that the specification (syllabus) requires you to study both areas of study prescribed for each year: Applied Music and Instrumental Music.

Applied Music 2012

- NAM 7: Stravinsky – *Pulcinella Suite*: 'Sinfonia', 'Gavotta' and 'Vivo'
- NAM 27: Gabrieli – *In ecclesiis*
- NAM 42: Auric – *Passport to Pimlico*: 'The Siege of Burgundy'
- NAM 46: Pheloung – *Morse on the Case*
- NAM 62: Mustapha Tettey Addy (Ghana) – *Agbekor Dance.*

Instrumental Music 2012

- NAM 3: Berlioz – *Harold in Italy*: movement III
- NAM 9: Shostakovich – String Quartet No. 8, Op. 110: movement I
- NAM 10: Cage – *Sonatas and Interludes for Prepared Piano*: Sonatas I–III
- NAM 15: Corelli – Trio Sonata in D, Op. 3 No. 2: movement IV
- NAM 20: Sweelinck – *Pavana Lachrimae*
- NAM 22: Mozart – Piano Sonata in B♭, K. 333: movement I
- NAM 58: Ram Narayan (India) – *Rag Bhairav*.

Applied Music 2013

- NAM 14: Gabrieli – *Sonata pian' e forte*
- NAM 28: J. S. Bach – Cantata No. 48, 'Ich elender Mensch': movements I–IV
- NAM 43: Bernstein – *On the Waterfront*: 'Symphonic Suite' (opening)
- NAM 44: Goldsmith – *Planet of the Apes*: 'The Hunt' (opening)
- NAM 59: Gong Kebyar de Sebatu (Bali) – *Baris Melampahan*.

Instrumental Music 2013

- NAM 5: Debussy – *Prélude à l'après-midi d'un faune*
- NAM 12: Reich – *New York Counterpoint*: movement II
- NAM 13: Holborne – Pavane 'The image of melancholy' and Galliard 'Ecce quam bonum'
- NAM 16: Haydn – String Quartet in E♭, Op. 33 No. 2, 'The Joke': movement IV
- NAM 18: Brahms – Piano Quintet in F minor, Op. 34: movement III
- NAM 19: Poulenc – Sonata for Horn, Trumpet and Trombone: movement I
- NAM 50: Miles Davis Quintet – *Four* (opening).

Applied Music 2014

➤ NAM 4: Wagner – Prelude to *Tristan und Isolde*

➤ NAM 26: Taverner – O Wilhelme, pastor bone

➤ NAM 29: Haydn – 'Quoniam tu solus' from *The Nelson Mass*

➤ NAM 47: Horner – *Titanic*: 'Take her to sea, Mr Murdoch'

➤ NAM 60: Red Stripe Ebony Steelband (Trinidad) – *Yellow Bird*.

Instrumental Music 2014

➤ NAM 1: J. S. Bach – Brandenburg Concerto No. 4 in G: movement I

➤ NAM 8: Webern – Quartet Op. 22: movement I

➤ NAM 17: Beethoven – Septet in E♭, Op. 20: movement I

➤ NAM 20: Sweelinck – *Pavana Lachrimae*

➤ NAM 23: Schumann – *Kinderscenen*, Op. 15: Nos 1, 3 and 11

➤ NAM 24: Debussy – *Pour le piano*: 'Sarabande'

➤ NAM 49: Duke Ellington and his Orchestra – *Black and Tan Fantasy.*

All works listed in both sections for each year must be tackled, as Section B (Music in Context) draws on the Applied Music list, and Section C (Continuity and Change) on the Instrumental Music list.

SECTION A (AURAL ANALYSIS)

There are two questions in this section of the examination:

1. Comparison of two excerpts of music without reference to notation

2. A general test of aural perception, involving notation of a melody (both pitch and rhythm), identifying specific compositional devices (keys, chords and cadences), and providing information on the historical context. For this question a skeleton score is provided.

You should practise as frequently and as regularly as possible, ensuring that you form the habit of:

•   Noting the number of marks there are (and therefore how much information is required) for each question, or part of question

•   Working out plausible possibilities (e.g. related keys) to support your impressions

- Understanding and using correct terminology (keep referring to the glossary at the end of this guide).

- In the comparison question, be prepared to answer questions on:

  - Instruments and/or voices
  - Textures
  - Rhythmic devices and patterns
  - Melodic aspects
  - Features of word-setting
  - Historical context (i.e. genre, composer, date of composition).

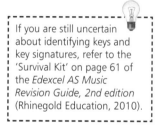

The historical context questions may well be multiple choice. If you are not sure about the genre, try to match the excerpts to the set works you have studied. Try hard, also, to relate the date of composition to the composer you have selected. If the question about the date is open-ended – i.e., you are invited to suggest a date yourself – try to be reasonably precise. For example, if you believe the composer is Bach, it is better to suggest '1720' rather than '18th century'.

> Useful resources are the Sample Assessment Materials (Edexcel, 2007, publications code UA018895) and *Edexcel A2 Music Listening Tests, 3rd edition* (Rhinegold Education, 2011).

Keys

Prediction of plausible possibilities could be especially helpful in the general test of aural perception. Before you hear the music played, use the skeleton score to identify the key at the opening, after which you can work out the five related keys (as specified in Edexcel's *Tutor Support Materials*) to which the music may modulate. Notice that the question will be restricted to just these possibilities.

> If you are still uncertain about identifying keys and key signatures, refer to the 'Survival Kit' on page 61 of the *Edexcel AS Music Revision Guide, 2nd edition* (Rhinegold Education, 2010).

The possibilities are as follows for an excerpt starting in a major key:

	Relative minor
Dominant	Relative minor of dominant
Subdominant	Relative minor of subdominant

For an excerpt starting in a minor key, the possibilities are:

	Relative major
Dominant	Relative major of dominant
Subdominant	Relative major of subdominant

In the case of music in the key of C major, for example, the range of possible modulations are:

	A minor (relative minor)
G major (dominant)	E minor (relative minor of the dominant)
F major (subdominant)	D minor (relative minor of the subdominant)

If the music is in C minor, the modulations will involve:

	E♭ major (relative major)
G minor (dominant)	B♭ major (relative major of the dominant)
F minor (subdominant)	A♭ major (relative major of the subdominant)

As a practice drill for this question, work out as quickly as possible the five related keys for all keys up to and including four sharps or flats (it is unlikely that a test involving more accidentals than this would be set in an exam).

Cadences

You are almost sure to be asked to identify cadences, especially in the general test of aural perception.

If you are not yet entirely confident about coping with cadences, try to remember the following points and develop a 'feel' for the effects they produce.

1. **Perfect** cadence: chord V–chord I

    There should be a closed or complete feel to the music at the point this cadence occurs. The key may have changed, of course, but whatever the context, the perfect cadence will give the impression of coming to the end of an individual statement, even though the music may move on. Such situations are perhaps analogous to the use of full stops part-way through a paragraph.

2. **Imperfect** cadence: finishes with chord V

    This cadence should give an open, incomplete feel, similar to a comma or semi-colon in a sentence.

3. **Interrupted** cadence: chord V–chord VI (most frequently)

    This is perhaps best regarded as a sort of derailed perfect cadence. Expectations are defeated by avoidance of the tonic, most frequently but not invariably through the use of chord VI.

4. **Plagal** cadence: chord IV–chord I

    Often likened to the church 'Amen', this results in a less emphatic return to the tonic chord, and is far less frequently heard.

Chords

The aural perception test can involve identification of any chord, but it is likely that at A2 level questions will involve some chromatic harmony. Study the numbered examples in the extract below from Mozart's Piano Sonata, K. 284. Remember, however, that it is really important that you not only recognise the chords on paper, but also that you develop the ability to recognise the sound of them. As ever, the context is all-important

Two different types of augmented 6th chord figure in these examples. We have named them here, but in the exam it is enough to describe them just as augmented 6ths.

(for example, it is frequently the case that the Neapolitan 6th substitutes for chord IIb preceding a cadence, just as augmented 6th chords often pave the way for a dominant chord or tonic chord in its second inversion).

1. (Italian) Augmented 6th chord. Note how it paves the way for progression Ic–V in D minor.

2. (German) Augmented 6th chord. Leading to Ic–V⁷–I in A minor.

3. Diminished 7ths on first and third crotchets of the bar.

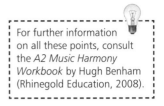

For further information on all these points, consult the *A2 Music Harmony Workbook* by Hugh Benham (Rhinegold Education, 2008).

4. Neapolitan 6th. Try to recognise the intensified plangent, 'weepy' sound.

5. (Italian) Augmented 6th preceding Ic–V⁷–I in D minor.

Other harmonic devices

You may also be asked to identify such common features as the following:

➤ Pedal point (you may have to state whether it is a tonic or dominant pedal)

➤ Suspension

➤ Appoggiatura

➤ False relation

➤ Tierce de Picardie.

See the glossary for definitions.

Finally, remember that in examinations you find yourself in an artificial situation. You are often tested on the various skills you learn separately, but in spite of this try not to let your own approach become rigidly compartmentalised. Try to appreciate musical works as a whole, and apply the knowledge you gain in one area of your activities to other aspects of your musical investigations. For example, your study of harmony should also help your listening and your exploration of musical styles.

SECTIONS B AND C

The rest of this guide is aimed at helping you to:

➤ Organise the information you have already collected (and may still be collecting)

➤ Focus on the demands of questions which are set in this exam

➤ Improve the way you express your ideas.

You must take an unmarked copy of the Anthology into the exam, and this in itself is a valuable aid to you if you can find your way round the scores quickly and efficiently. It will help if you **keep listening to your prescribed works** so that you begin to recognise and locate the key features we shall be looking at. Obviously, it makes much more sense to be able to locate features you require in the score itself than to try to memorise abstract accounts of the work.

Demands of Sections B and C

In Section B, you answer two out of three options, all dealing with music in context. In other words, the questions will involve showing how features of musical style relate to the historical background or the purpose of the work. The works are all taken from the Applied Music list, and by definition have some sort of function (e.g. incidental music, music for opera, or music for some sort of ceremony).

In Section B you may answer in note form if you prefer, without the risk of incurring any penalty. Each option is worth 13 marks, giving a total of 26 for the section. Do not waste time answering a third option as well – you won't gain any more marks, and may not leave yourself enough time to produce a well-written essay for Section C.

In Section C, you must answer one question of the two set on Instrumental Music. You should write in continuous prose, as your essay will be assessed both for the information it contains and the way you have expressed yourself.

The total mark for the essay is 36, and we shall see how the marks are allocated in the sample essays that can be found towards the end of this book.

In Edexcel's Sample Assessment Materials you will find holistic descriptors for each question set in both Sections B and C. The examiners will naturally take into account the number of correct, relevant and valid points you make. They will also assess the quality of the writing (Quality of Written Communication – QWC), and this will involve such aspects as:

> The holistic descriptors are based on a hierarchy of words – from 'Outstanding' to 'Poor' – each with a range of marks and a brief description of the attributes expected in an answer at that level.

➢ Organisation, planning and coherence

➢ Syntax and spelling

➢ Use of appropriate terminology.

We have already stated that you may answer in note form in Section B if you wish. You will, however, have to be careful to express yourself as clearly as possible, arranging your points in a logical, coherent sequence.

On pages 14–80 are **revision notes** for each of the set works, giving a brief historical context, followed by a series of pointers to the most important technical features of the music: rhythm and metre, melody, harmony, tonality, texture, performance resources and structure.

We have also provided examples of **questions, mark schemes (indicative content) and specimen answers with commentaries** for you to study. Some answers have been left unmarked for you to evaluate. In addition we have suggested short exercises aimed at helping you to improve the way you present your ideas. Naturally, you will be most interested in the set works for your year, but find time to glance at the remaining specimen answers, as suggestions are made throughout this section on how to improve the quality of your written communication.

One of the most common reasons for losing marks is irrelevance. Always stick to the point and write about the works specified in the question.

Do not worry if, sometimes, you seem to be stating the obvious! And, where possible, always try to provide at least one example for each point you make, though in some cases more than one example would be desirable. For example, if the question concerns tonality then you should try to give as much detail as possible about how the composer modulates right the way through the piece. Many candidates fail to earn high marks because they neglect to pursue the line of enquiry as thoroughly as possible.

Think about how best to organise your time when answering questions. You do not have to worry about Section A, as the instructions and extracts on the CD dictate timings for you. For the rest of the paper, for which you will probably have approximately an hour and a half, you could allow yourself roughly 20 minutes for each of the sub-sections you select in Section B, and about 50 minutes for the Section C essay. Try to allow some time for reading through your work before handing in your answer book.

Useful additional reading:

➤ *Dictionary of Music in Sound* by David Bowman (Rhinegold Education, 2002)

➤ *Writing about Music Workbook* by Alistair Wightman (Rhinegold Education, 2008)

➤ *Edexcel A2 Music Study Guide* by David Bowman and Paul Terry (Rhinegold Education, 2009).

Revision notes

Below, we have provided a series of points that should help you to focus on the most important aspects of each of the works set for the year in which you are taking the examination. It would not be wise to try to memorise everything for a parrot-like recitation of facts and figures. We suggest you check that you understand the main points, or generalisations, given under the various headings. After this, try to absorb some of the additional points – these should help you to think of your own examples which can be used to illustrate the work in question.

It is most important that you keep referring to the Anthology, and associate the points made in the following lists with **what you hear in the music and see on the score**. Attempting to learn these points in the form of abstract crib notes means you do not get anything out of the exercise in the long term, and also run the risk of error.

We have also made one or two suggestions for further listening. While by no means essential, it would help you to broaden your acquaintance with the composer or type of music in question, and hopefully aid you in the listening section of the examination.

APPLIED MUSIC 2012

Stravinsky – *Pulcinella Suite*: 'Sinfonia', 'Gavotta' and 'Vivo'

Background	<ul><li>First performed on 15 May 1920 at the Paris Opéra</li><li>Commissioned by Serge Diaghilev, the impresario who founded the Ballets Russes</li><li>In contrast to the huge orchestral demands of the ballet scores of the years preceding World War I (such as *Petrushka* and *The Rite of Spring*), *Pulcinella's* relatively modest demands are indicative of the reduced scale of Diaghilev's post-war enterprises.</li><li>This work is neoclassical in style:<ul><li>It reflects a reaction against the emotionalism and 'giganticism' of late-Romantic music</li><li>It uses 18th-century models</li><li>The Sinfonia is based on music by Gallo</li><li>The Gavotta is extracted from keyboard variations by Monza</li><li>The Vivo is built on a cello sonata by Pergolesi.</li></ul></li><li>Stravinsky goes further than arranging his 18th-century materials; instead, though retaining the broad outlines of the originals, he 'recomposes' them.</li></ul>

Rhythm and metre	The basic rhythmic schemes and metres are disrupted by:
	• Heavy off-beat accents (e.g. Vivo, bar 33)
	• Persistent syncopation (e.g. Sinfonia, bars 17–18 in violin II)
	• Bars with differing time signatures (e.g. Sinfonia, bars 10–12)
	• Introduction of long sustained notes at odds with 'foreground' music (e.g. Sinfonia, bars 7–9)
	• Irregular groupings of shorter notes (e.g. Gavotta, groups of 5 (bar 27), 9 (bar 31), 11 (bar 73), 12 (bar 78)).
Melody	Compared to the other musical elements, melody is more recognisably similar to the original sources, although Stravinsky does introduce:
	• Blurred outlines through glissandi (e.g. Vivo, bar 2, trombone)
	• Extensive 'non-Baroque' ornamentation (e.g. Gavotta, bar 83, flute 1).
Harmony	Disruptions here include:
	• The introduction of additional notes to result in 'wrong-note' harmony (e.g. the added 9th in the violin II part in bar 3 of the Sinfonia)
	• The combination of G and D major chords at bar 44 (beat 1) of the Gavotta
	• A loud tonic-over-dominant chord at bar 33 of the Vivo:
	• Use of folk-style drones in unexpected contexts (e.g. Sinfonia, violin II, bars 17–18)
	• Weakening of bass lines (e.g. Sinfonia, bar 43 – sudden drop in volume and removal of double bass from the texture)
	• Unexpected cadences (e.g. III–I at end of the Vivo).
Texture and scoring	The original pieces were taken from chamber music or keyboard sources, thus allowing considerable freedom in orchestration and texture:
	• There is no continuo
	• The solo quintet in the Sinfonia and Vivo may have been suggested by the Baroque concerto grosso (but if so is a highly unusual 'concertino' grouping)
	• The solo trombone in the Vivo, with glissandi, is a 20th-century touch
	• As is the high double-bass solo in the Vivo

	• The Gavotta is scored for wind instruments only, reflecting Stravinsky's increasing preference for such sonorities (e.g. *Symphonies for Wind Instruments*, *Concerto for Piano and Winds*).
	Textures, though predominantly melody-dominated homophony, are highly contrasting:
	• Loosely imitative wind writing at bars 6–10 of the Sinfonia
	• Melody and drone at bars 17–18 of the Sinfonia
	• Sustained chords in the solo quintet, supported by repeated chords in the main part of the orchestra (bars 37–39 of the Sinfonia)
	• Two-part oboe and horn writing at the start of Variation I of the Gavotta
	• Quasi-Alberti bass in the bassoons in Variation II
	• Unison statement of the main theme at start of the Vivo
	• Heterophony between flutes and trumpet from bar 38 of the Vivo.

> Alberti bass is a particular form of broken-chord accompaniment in which the figuration consists of a recurring four-note pattern in the order low-high-middle-high:

Structure and tonality	• These aspects of the music afford the clearest evidence of its stylistic origins in the 18th century
	• The Sinfonia is in rounded binary form (with the A section as bars 1–15 and B section bars 16–44); or else it is an abbreviated ritornello form, with the ritornello theme appearing at bar 1 in G, bar 16 in D, and bar 35 in G
	• Modulations to B minor (bar 26), E minor (bar 29) and A minor (bar 31), as well as use of the circle of 5ths progression, are as expected in 18th-century music
	• The Gavotta is in binary form, and goes on to include only two of the six variations Monza wrote
	• The first part modulates from D to A (bar 10), then to G (bar 14), then briefly through A (bar 18), F♯ minor (bar 20), E minor (bar 22), then to D (bar 24 to the end)
	• The Vivo is in rounded binary form, with modulations from F to C at the end of the first section (bar 21), and to the tonic minor (bar 46)
	• Stravinsky departs from the original by inserting three bars at the start of the second section (bars 22–24).
Further listening	• The rest of the *Pulcinella Suite*
	• *Symphony of Psalms*: movement III (NAM 31)
	• *Petrushka* (an example of Stravinsky's early Russian nationalist style).

Gabrieli – *In Ecclesiis*

Background	• *In ecclesiis* was published in 1615 in *Symphoniae Sacrae*
	• It was probably intended for performance in San Marco (St Mark's Cathedral), Venice, where Gabrieli was organist. But it may also have been performed in other Venetian churches, notably San Rocco, where Gabrieli also worked as organist
	• It is a motet (i.e. a work, typically with Latin text, intended for a specific occasion or day in the church calendar, and not part of the Mass)
	• In its general style *In ecclesiis* mainly shows early Baroque traits, though some features are also to be found in Renaissance music
	• It was clearly intended for performance in one of the best-endowed churches in one of the wealthiest states of the period, as shown by the large performing forces consisting of:
	• The large accompanying instrumental band
	• Use of four soloists
	• Choir
	• Organ continuo.
Rhythm and metre	• In quadruple time ($\frac{4}{2}$) alternating with brief, dancing triple-time ($\frac{3}{2}$) sections
	• Towards the end there are passages, notated in $\frac{3}{1}$, with long note values to create a sense of majesty and awe
	• There is considerable rhythmic variety to project the sense of the text:
	• Long note values (e.g. to emphasise the word 'Deus' at bar 102)
	• Lively dotted rhythms (e.g. bar 32)
	• Florid, rapidly moving lines (e.g. bar 68)
	• Syncopation (e.g. bar 17).
Melody and word-setting	• Often stepwise, and with a relatively narrow range, even in the solo parts (e.g. first countertenor solo spans an octave, but the first baritone solo only a major 6th)
	• Frequent repetition of phrases (e.g. bars 3–5)
	• Sequence (e.g. descending at bars 13–16; ascending at bars 17–19)
	• Declamatory style, evident in use of:
	• Syllabic style for clarity (e.g. bars 39–44, alto and tenor solo parts)
	• Prolonged virtuoso melisma (bars 68 and 116–117):
	De - - - - - us

Harmony	• The older, Renaissance-derived style is evident in the frequent cadences on varying degrees of the scale, use of suspensions and the consonant 4th at some cadences

• The ending is marked by a series of perfect cadences, followed by a plagal cadence

• The daring Baroque features include:

  • An augmented triad (bar 31, third beat with a clash between E and F):

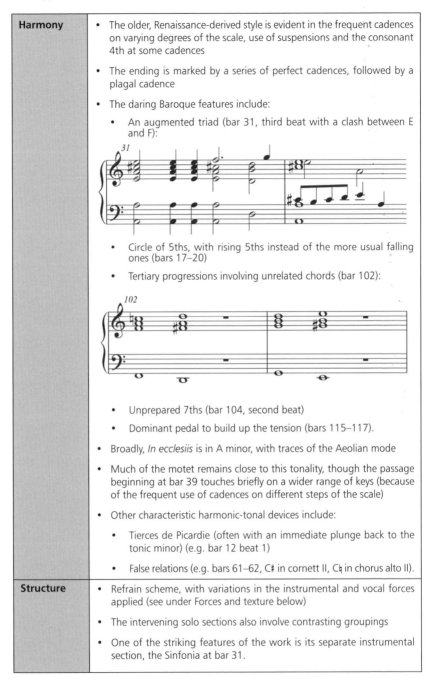

  • Circle of 5ths, with rising 5ths instead of the more usual falling ones (bars 17–20)

  • Tertiary progressions involving unrelated chords (bar 102):

  • Unprepared 7ths (bar 104, second beat)

  • Dominant pedal to build up the tension (bars 115–117).

• Broadly, *In ecclesiis* is in A minor, with traces of the Aeolian mode

• Much of the motet remains close to this tonality, though the passage beginning at bar 39 touches briefly on a wider range of keys (because of the frequent use of cadences on different steps of the scale)

• Other characteristic harmonic-tonal devices include:

  • Tierces de Picardie (often with an immediate plunge back to the tonic minor) (e.g. bar 12 beat 1)

  • False relations (e.g. bars 61–62, C♯ in cornett II, C♮ in chorus alto II).

Structure	• Refrain scheme, with variations in the instrumental and vocal forces applied (see under Forces and texture below)

• The intervening solo sections also involve contrasting groupings

• One of the striking features of the work is its separate instrumental section, the Sinfonia at bar 31.

Forces and texture	• Besides the four vocal soloists (countertenor, alto, tenor and bass) and the chorus (alto I, alto II, tenor and bass), Gabrieli required an instrumental group of three cornetts, violin (corresponding in range to the modern viola) and two trombones. In addition there was the continuo part (basso per l'organo).

• A range of textures is used throughout the work:

  • Monody (e.g. bars 1–5)

  • Homophony (e.g. bar 102)

  • Imitation (e.g. bars 10–11, alto 1 and tenor)

  • Canon (notably from bar 114)

  • Antiphony (e.g. bars 6–10, chorus and countertenor solo).

• The contrasting of available forces is characteristic of early-Baroque concertato style:

Bars	Forces
1–5	Vocal solo (countertenor)
6–12	Refrain (chorus and countertenor)
13–24	Vocal solo (baritone)
25–31	Refrain (chorus and baritone)
31–38	Sinfonia
39–61	Alto and tenor with instrumental group
62–68	Refrain (tenor, alto, chorus and instrumental group)
68–94	Countertenor and baritone with continuo only
95–101	Refrain (countertenor, baritone and chorus)
102–118	Tutti
119–129	Extended refrain (tutti)

Further listening	• Gabrieli – *Sonata pian' e forte* (NAM 14)
	• Monteverdi – *Vespers*.

Auric – *Passport to Pimlico*: 'The Siege of Burgundy'

Background	• Incidental music for one of the 'Ealing' comedies
	
	• During the 1920s, Auric was a member of *Les Six*, with Poulenc, Milhaud, Honegger, Taillefaire and Durey. They strived for simplicity, terseness and clarity, and embraced new popular styles
	
	• Auric's reputation now rests on ballet scores (some for Diaghilev) and film music, including such classics as *La belle et la bête* (Cocteau and Delannoy) and *Orphée* (Cocteau)
	
	The 'Ealing' comedies, dating from the late 1940s and early 1950s, were so-called because of the location of the film studio where they were produced. Auric also provided scores for *The Lavender Hill Mob* (1951) and *The Titfield Thunderbolt* (1952).
	
	• In this excerpt, the comic aspects of the scene are conveyed by:
	    • Rapid changes of thematic material
	    • Speedy changes of key
	    • Colourful and apt orchestration.

Rhythm and metre	• The material is integrated within the prevailing quadruple pulse, with only one change of time signature ($\frac{3}{4}$ at bar 51), and one significant change of tempo (*più andante* at bar 20) • Throughout much of the excerpt there is a motor rhythm of semiquavers • Rhythmic diminution is applied at bar 3.
Melody	• Two and four-bar phrases dominate • Largely diatonic with occasional chromatic alterations (e.g. bar 22) • Ornamentation (trills and grace notes) • Frequent use of scales • Relatively limited note ranges.
Harmony	Auric uses a basically functional harmonic language. The most notable features are: • Frequent perfect cadences • Added-note harmony (final cadence) • Occasional whole-tone harmony (bar 27) • Augmented 6th (bar 26) • Parallel triads (e.g. bars 47–48) and parallelism in general (e.g. in contrary motion at bar 8) • Pedals (e.g. bars 21–25) • 7th chords of various sorts (e.g. bar 58).

Tonality	• Changes of key are usually sudden • With frequent use of tertiary relationships, the main landmarks are:

Bars	Key
1	E major
9	G major
15	B minor/major
21	E major
33	C major
39	E♭ major
43	E major
55	C major

Texture and orchestration	• The music is notated in short score with added indications regarding instrumentation • Auric required a moderate-sized orchestra with celeste, glockenspiel and percussion • Strings are sometimes played pizzicato • Muted trumpet is required (bar 41) • The bright opening has trills in the wind • Low tremolandi are used (bar 52) • There is considerable variety in texture, the main features being:

Bars	Texture
5	Essentially melody-dominated homophony, with the melody doubled at the 5th and octave and accompanied by parallel 3rds
9	Texture enlivened by countermelodies
15	Octaves in the bass, then dialogue between the strings and wind
21	Melody in the bass with rapidly repeated chords in the upper strings
46	Homorhythm

Further listening	• Poulenc – *Sonata for Horn, Trumpet and Trombone*: movement I (NAM 19).

Pheloung – *Morse on the Case*

Background	• The excerpt is taken from an episode in a long-running series of 'police procedural' crime dramas
	
	• The music is designed to be both atmospheric and unobtrusive
	
	• The essential effects are obtained through:
	
	   • Limited resources (here only strings, harp, piano, four horns and oboe)
	
	   • Limited rhythmic movement, a characteristic feature of Pheloung's style in the *Morse* music being lengthy, sustained notes
	
	   • The slowly evolving development of a small number of motifs.

Rhythm and metre	• Though notated throughout in $\frac{4}{4}$, the metre is not detectable because of the lengthy, pulseless sounds and seemingly unpredictable placing of motifs within bars • On paper, it is possible to see irregular diminution of motifs, although this process is difficult to identify aurally • A silent bar (bars 60–61) further intensifies the sense of lack of motion.

Melody	• This extract, like many other passages of incidental music in *Inspector Morse*, relies on the use of short motifs
	
	• The main motivic/melodic features here are:
	
	   • Use of the Aeolian mode, except for F♯ (bar 52 and elsewhere) and A♭ (bar 92)
	
	   • Gradual unfolding of lines built of perfect 4ths, minor 3rds and major 2nds
	
	• The component intervals are treated in various ways, being:
	
	   • Inverted
	   • Verticalised
	   • Rhythmically diminished
	   • Fragmented.

Diminution

Augmentation and inversion

Verticalisation

Harmony and tonality	• There is no sense of functional progression in this excerpt
	• 'Harmony' consists mainly of verticalisations of the component intervals
	• It is therefore mildly dissonant
	• The chromatic notes, especially A♭, produce more stringent clashes, with A♭ in oboe and A♮ in viola at bars 93–94
	• The excerpt eventually moves to a C major chord (bar 110)
	• But the F♯s, e.g. bars 105 and 108, perhaps suggest the Lydian mode
	• The final chord is ambiguous as it lacks the 3rd.
Structure	• There is no discernible structure
	• The excerpt appears to be through-composed to reflect the on-screen events.
Texture	• Pheloung avoids tutti passages, preferring to contrast densities of sound and timbre
	• Harp doesn't appear until bar 101
	• Upper strings play throughout, but cellos and bass don't appear until bar 99
	• Piano plays intermittently throughout, playing variously single notes, two notes, parallel 9ths (bar 36) and four notes on one occasion (bar 98)

	• The four horns are only used together from bar 98 • The piano has the most rhythmically active part.
Further listening	• By way of contrast, try Patrick Gowers' incidental music to the 1984–94 TV series *Sherlock Holmes*.

Mustapha Tettey Addy (Ghana) – *Agbekor Dance*

Background	• *Agbekor Dance* originated with the Ewe people of Ghana • The version in the anthology is a transcription as the music is performed without notation. • It was a ritual war dance, but now is performed at social events or cultural displays • The dance is characterised by stylised movements which symbolise the various stages of battle • It is played on percussion instruments only, and so the only musical aspects that are relevant here are timbre, rhythm and structure.
Instruments	There are three instruments: 1. Gankogui – a double bell, made of iron, struck with beaters. The bells sound approximately an octave apart 2. Atsimevu – the master drum, a relatively tall, narrow drum, played variously with one or two beaters, or else with the hand, so producing various muting effects that simulate speech rhythms. It is used to give cues to the other performers 3. Sogo – a barrel-shaped drum, played with beaters.
Rhythm	• *Agbekor Dance* is polyrhythmic and involves cross-rhythms • The gankogui plays an ostinato throughout • This ostinato is a timeline to which the other parts relate • Although the time signature is $\frac{12}{8}$, the gankogui's part consists of an additive rhythm of 2+3+2+2+3 quavers, giving a syncopated effect • The sogo has a separate rhythm, with muting giving the impression of two pitches • It opens with steady, uninterrupted quavers, but eventually semiquavers and dotted rhythms are introduced • The atsimevu opens with steady dotted-crotchet beats, played on the wood of the drum, before introducing a wider range of rhythmic figures and groupings (e.g. semiquavers, quavers (sometimes in sets of four) and triplets) • At bar 21, the atsimevu doubles the ostinato.

Structure	• This element of the piece is based largely upon repetition, evolution and elaboration of basic rhythmic patterns • In effect it is through-composed.

INSTRUMENTAL MUSIC 2012

Berlioz – *Harold in Italy*: movement III

Background	• First performed in 1834 • A work for solo viola and orchestra, commissioned by Nicolo Paganini, the leading virtuoso violinist of the day • Paganini, however, never performed it on the grounds that the solo part was not sufficiently difficult • This excerpt is the third movement of a four-movement symphony • The symphony is programmatic – it depicts a poem by Lord Byron • The work features the idée fixe technique already used by Berlioz in *Symphonie fantastique* (1830) • The idée fixe here symbolises the character of Harold and appears in all movements • In this movement it is heard first at bar 65 in the solo viola.
Rhythm and metre	• The movement opens with $\frac{6}{8}$ saltarello dance rhythms, with frequent dotted rhythms and stresses on the second beat of the bar: • The second section (bar 32) is in a slower $\frac{6}{8}$ with some bars appearing to be in $\frac{3}{4}$ (e.g. bars 37 and 38):

	• The idée fixe stands out from the rest of the texture as it is in longer notes, chiefly dotted minims • Unusual simultaneous presentation of all rhythmic elements occurs at bar 166 • Augmentation is used near the end of the extract (bars 192–193).
Melody	There are several distinct melodies: 1. Saltarello (bar 1) • One-bar cells, resulting in phrases of various, irregular lengths • Narrow range at first, later expanding to a 9th • Revolves around E • Mainly moves by step or by 3rds • Involves repetition, sequence and inversion • Modal elements hint at a folk influence • As do the ornaments. 2. Serenade (bar 32) • Opens with a broken-chord figure • Phrase lengths are irregular. 3. Idée fixe (bar 65) • Characteristic falling 3rd and 6th • Broken chords.
Harmony	• Functional, with cadences • Characteristic features include: • A double pedal (drone) in the saltarello to produce a folk-music effect • Secondary 7ths (e.g. bar 74) • Diminished 7ths (e.g. bar 41) • Chromaticism (e.g. bar 44).
Tonality	• C major, with only occasional modulation (e.g. G major at bars 89–90, D minor at bar 100).
Structure	Broadly a ternary form: • Saltarello – Allegro assai (1–31) • Serenade – Allegretto (32–135) • Saltarello – Allegro assai (136–165) • Coda, combining all melodic material – Allegretto (166–208).

Resources and texture	• Viola solo and symphony orchestra
	• Notice the transposing instruments:
	• Cor anglais, sounding a perfect 5th below written pitch
	• Horn in F, sounding a perfect 5th below written pitch
	• Horn in E, sounding a minor 6th below written pitch.
	The absence of valve horns points to a date of composition relatively early in the 19th century.
	• Other unusual additions for this period include the harp and the piccolo (which sounds an octave higher than written pitch)
	• The texture is broadly melody-dominated homophony
	• Noteworthy devices include:
	• Drone in the saltarello section (from bar 1)
	• Divided orchestral violas
	• Octave doubling in the woodwind section (piccolo and oboe from bar 4)
	• Broken-chord accompaniment in clarinet (e.g. bars 48–52)
	• Double-stopping in solo viola (from bar 72)
	• Harp harmonics, doubling flute (from bar 167)
	• Monophonic writing for solo viola near the end (bar 202).
Further listening	• Berlioz – *Symphonie fantastique*
	• Berlioz – *Le carnaval romain*.

Shostakovich – String Quartet No. 8, Op. 110: movement I

Background	• Composed in 1960 following the composer's enforced membership of the Communist Party in Russia, and a visit to Dresden where it was possible still to observe the effects of bombing during World War II
	• The quartet is intensely autobiographical, with extensive use of the motif D–Eb–C–B, a musical cipher which stands for an abbreviated form of the composer's name (DSCH – Dmitri Schostakowitsch in German transliteration), as well as quotations from some of his earlier works.
Rhythm and metre	• Slow (Largo) simple quadruple time throughout
	• No values shorter than a quaver, many very much longer
	• Some dotted rhythms.

Melody	• In a low tessitura throughout
	• Melodies are often chromatic
	• Prominence is given to the DSCH motif
	• Some melodic material is taken from earlier works (e.g. Symphony No. 1 at bar 19)
	• Appoggiaturas (e.g. bar 30)
	• Conjunct movement (e.g. from bar 55)
	• Some narrow-range motifs (bars 59–60 in violin II)
	• Repetitive figures (bars 50–56 in the violins)
	• Sequence (bars 19–23 in the viola).
Harmony	• Some clearly defined, traditional progressions (e.g. a perfect cadence at bar 26, with a suspension, preceded by V–Ib–IV):
	• Less traditional chord progressions (e.g. bars 79–81 consist of G major, E♭ minor, F major, with chromatic inner parts)
	• There are also passages of harmonic stasis (i.e. no progression as such) e.g. the drone at bar 28, tonic pedal on C at bar 50, then dominant pedal at bar 67.
Tonality	• The tonal scheme is slow moving, starting in C minor, with a quasi-fugal answer in G minor/dominant (bar 2), and hints of F minor at bar 7
	• The structure is defined partly by perfect cadences (in C minor) at bars 26, 84 and 122
	• Other devices used to reinforce the tonality are the drone (on tonic and dominant) at bars 28–45 and tonic pedal at bars 50–66
	• There is a major mode inflection at bar 55, a shift to A minor at bar 87, F♯ minor at bar 93, C major at bar 95, and a return to C minor at bar 105. The G♯ at the end prepares for the second movement.

Structure	The music unfolds without reference to traditional forms, though Shostakovich reprises some passages. Keys are clearly established through cadences and drones or pedals.

Bars	Section	Key
1–27	Section A, closing with DSCH	C minor
28–45	Section B	C minor (drone)
46–49	Link (using DSCH)	C minor
50–78	Section C, with reharmonisation of DSCH	C minor
79–104	Developed recapitulation of A and B	A minor (bar 87), C major (bar 95)
105–118	Based on bars 11–23	C minor
118–124	Final reference to DSCH	C minor
125–126	Link to second movement	Unison G♯

Texture	This movement for traditional string quartet exploits low tessituras throughout and draws on a variety of textures, such as:

Bars	Texture
1–11	Four-part imitation
11–13	DSCH in octaves with internal pedal in viola
19–22	Two-part counterpoint
23–27	Homophony
28–44	Drone with melody in violin I
50–78	Pedal supporting accompanying figures and melody
87–91	Chord in upper parts with melody in cello
92–94	Four-part free counterpoint

Further listening	• Shostakovich – Prelude and Fugue in A, Op. 87 No. 7 (NAM 25) • Shostakovich – Symphony No. 5, Op. 47.

Cage – Sonatas and Interludes for Prepared Piano: Sonatas I–III

Background	• The Sonatas are taken from a cycle of 16 sonatas and four interludes, completed in 1948 • They are one of a series of works written for prepared piano (see instructions preceding the Sonatas in the Anthology for information on how the piano is 'prepared') • The prepared piano originated when Cage was commissioned to compose a dance piece for Syvilla Fort in 1940

	• The performing venue was so restricted that Cage could only use a piano, and therefore had to expand on the range of sounds available to him from the one instrument he could use
	• The works of these years also reflect the composer's interest in Indian philosophy, and the idea of the 'permanent emotions'
	• Because of preparation, the most important musical elements for the listener involve rhythm, structure, texture and timbre.
Rhythm and metre	• With the fractal/micro-macrocosmic scheme, small-scale rhythmic durations determine the overall proportions of the structure

Rhythm and metre (continued)

• Sonata I uses seven-crotchet units in sets of 4–1–3 (repeated) and 4–2 (repeated):

Bars 1–7	4 x 7 = duration of 28 crotchets
Bar 8	1 x 7 = duration of 7 crotchets
Bars 9–12	3 x 7 = duration of 21 crotchets
Bars 13–19	4 x 7 = duration of 28 crotchets
Bars 20–26	2 x 7 = 14 crotchets

• Sonata II uses 31-crotchet units in sets of 1½ (repeated) and 2⅜ (repeated):

Bars 1–14	1½ x 31 = duration of 46½ crotchets
Bars 15–37	2⅜ x 31 = duration of 53½ crotchets (approximately)

• Sonata III uses 34-crotchet units in sets of 1 (repeated) and 3¼ (repeated):

Bars 1–8	1 x 34 = duration of 34 crotchets
Bars 9–32	3¼ x 34 = duration of 110½ crotchets

• At surface level, the Sonatas are marked by:

  • Off-beat effects

  • Triplets

  • Other irregular note groupings

  • Rhythmic displacements of short patterns (although Sonata III makes use of a more regular pulse)

• There are frequent changes of time signature.

Melody	• The usual features of melody are difficult to discern because of the distortion of pitch through the piano's preparations
	• There are some apparently chromatic and pentatonic elements
	• Elsewhere, lines are often angular.

Harmony	• Traditional harmonic procedures are impossible because of the effects of preparation
	• There are no cadences, and only occasional discernible chord structures:
	• The opening 7th chord of Sonata I
	• The parallel chords at bars 20–23 of Sonata I.
Tonality	• It is not useful to speak of tonality in relation to these works, although Cage occasionally uses procedures which have a tonal function in traditional music – e.g. the pedal in the left-hand part at the opening of Sonata III, notated as an A but usually sounding as C.
Structure	• The Sonatas are superficially in binary form with repeats and some recapitulation (e.g. Sonata I, bar 18)
	• The organisation is fundamentally rhythmic (see above).
Texture and timbre	• Preparation changes timbres drastically, leading to 'dead' toneless sounds and various distortions of pitched sounds
	• The effect is often likened to gamelan
	• Textures vary from:
	• Homophonic (e.g. Sonata I bar 1)
	• Monophonic (e.g. Sonata II bar 1)
	• Two-part homorhythmic (e.g. Sonata II bar 10)
	• Layered (e.g. Sonata II bar 30)
	• Melody with pedal (e.g. Sonata III bars 1–8).
Further listening	• Cage – *Amores.*

Corelli – Trio Sonata in D, Op. 3 No. 2: movement IV

Background	• Published in 1689, and therefore standing on the borderline between middle and late Baroque
	• The last movement of a four-movement sonata
	• One of a set of 12 trio sonatas
	• Although described as a trio sonata, the work requires four players: two violins, violone (the equivalent of a cello) and organ continuo
	• The organ supplies harmonies as indicated by the figured bass
	• The use of the organ has led to the piece's designation as a sonata di chiesa (church sonata), but it can be performed with any suitable continuo instrument (e.g. harpsichord), and in any performance venue.

Rhythm and metre	• In rapid compound duple time ($\frac{6}{8}$), in the style of a gigue
	• Basic motif is made up of quavers and semiquavers, with occasional longer notes in the upper parts
	• Syncopation at bars 26–27
	• Feeling of $\frac{3}{4}$ in bar 27 arising from a hemiola:
Melody	• Basic motif composed of 3rds and stepwise movement
	• Inversion at bar 20
	• Sequence at bars 8–10.
Harmony	• Functional
	• Diatonic, with chords mainly in root position and first inversion
	• Perfect cadences
	• Suspensions
	• Inverted pedals (e.g. bars 15–18, violin II).
Tonality	• D major, with modulations to related keys, e.g.:
	• A major at bar 19
	• B minor at bars 27–28
	• E minor at bars 31–32.
Structure	• Binary, with each section repeated.
Texture	• Writing for the violin is idiomatic, though Corelli tends to avoid the lowest registers and anything above third position
	• The texture is often 'polarised', i.e. two high violin parts and a low bass line
	• This movement is broadly contrapuntal with fugal elements, although the writing is also frequently homorhythmic (e.g. bars 3–4)
	• Stretto is used at bar 20, where the imitation comes after one bar only.
Further listening	• Corelli – any concerto grosso or trio sonata.

Sweelinck – *Pavana Lachrimae*

Background	• *Pavana Lachrimae* (1615) was a transcription with variations on the lute-song *Flow my tears* by John Dowland (NAM 33) • It was probably intended for performance on harpsichord, and provides evidence of the transfer of English virginalist techniques to the continent • The pavan is a relatively slow dance in three sections.
Rhythm and metre	• Notated in common time • Occasional syncopation.
Melody	• Transfer of vocal styles to keyboard with extensive conjunct movement • the descending (falling tears) line spanning a perfect 4th is sometimes changed to span a diminished 4th (e.g. C–G♯ in bars 3–4): 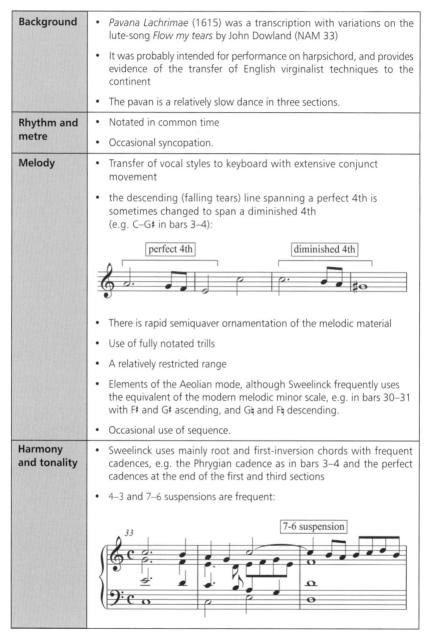 • There is rapid semiquaver ornamentation of the melodic material • Use of fully notated trills • A relatively restricted range • Elements of the Aeolian mode, although Sweelinck frequently uses the equivalent of the modern melodic minor scale, e.g. in bars 30–31 with F♯ and G♯ ascending, and G♮ and F♮ descending. • Occasional use of sequence.
Harmony and tonality	• Sweelinck uses mainly root and first-inversion chords with frequent cadences, e.g. the Phrygian cadence as in bars 3–4 and the perfect cadences at the end of the first and third sections • 4–3 and 7–6 suspensions are frequent:

Harmony and tonality	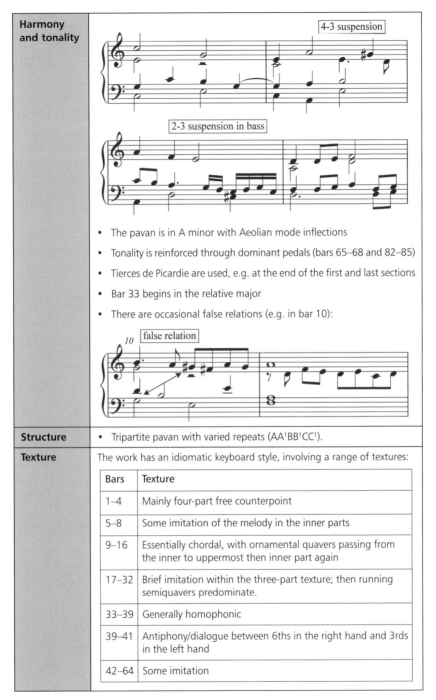

- The pavan is in A minor with Aeolian mode inflections
- Tonality is reinforced through dominant pedals (bars 65–68 and 82–85)
- Tierces de Picardie are used, e.g. at the end of the first and last sections
- Bar 33 begins in the relative major
- There are occasional false relations (e.g. in bar 10):

Structure	• Tripartite pavan with varied repeats (AA¹BB¹CC¹).
Texture	The work has an idiomatic keyboard style, involving a range of textures:

Bars	Texture
1–4	Mainly four-part free counterpoint
5–8	Some imitation of the melody in the inner parts
9–16	Essentially chordal, with ornamental quavers passing from the inner to uppermost then inner part again
17–32	Brief imitation within the three-part texture; then running semiquavers predominate.
33–39	Generally homophonic
39–41	Antiphony/dialogue between 6ths in the right hand and 3rds in the left hand
42–64	Some imitation

Further listening	• Holborne – Pavane *The image of melancholy* (NAM 13) • Dowland – *Flow my tears* (NAM 33) • Sweelinck – any set of variations.

Mozart – Piano Sonata in B♭, K. 333: movement I

Background	• The first movement of a Classical three-movement sonata • Intended as much for domestic/instructional purposes as concert use • Composed in 1783.
Rhythm and metre	• In simple quadruple (common) time • There is syncopation in the first subject, and more of a tendency for continuous semiquaver movement in the later stages of the second subject, so providing increased momentum.
Melody	• There is typically Classical periodic phrasing at the opening of the second subject • In contrast, the first subject consists of a four-bar phrase, answered by a six-bar passage • The movement opens diatonically, but chromatic inflections are frequent • Melodies are often extended by use of sequence • Ornamentation includes appoggiaturas (both diatonic and chromatic) and turns.

Harmony	• Functional, with cadences
	
	• Mozart uses the typically Classical cadential 6–4
	
	• Other noteworthy features are:
	
	  • Appoggiatura chords (e.g. bar 63)
	
	  • Diminished 7th chords (e.g. bar 69)
	
	  • Augmented 6th chords (e.g. bar 80):

Tonality	• Clearly defined, with modulations that delineate the structure.

Structure	The movement is in sonata form:

1–63	Exposition	
1–10	First subject	B♭ major
10–22	Transition	B♭ major
23–63	Second subject with codetta	F major
63–93	Development	Various: F major/F minor/C minor/B♭ major/G minor/dominant preparation for…
93–165	Recapitulation (With second subject at bar 119, now in tonic rather than dominant)	B♭ major

Resources	• Early wooden-framed piano (fortepiano) with a five-octave range, as opposed to harpsichord.
Texture	• Various forms of melody-dominated homophony, with the right hand carrying the melody throughout • Lean textures, often consisting of only two lines, the left hand using a broken-chord accompaniment (or occasionally Alberti bass) • The densest chords occur at the start of the second subject (to emphasise the tonality at these points) • Very occasionally the right hand plays octaves.
Further listening	• Mozart – Piano Concerto No. 21 in C, K. 467.

Ram Narayan (India) – *Rag Bhairav*

Background	• *Rag Bhairav* is an example of north Indian music • It is similar to the chamber music of the Western classical tradition in that it is performed to a relatively small audience • This rag is traditionally performed in the hour immediately following sunrise • The term 'rag' refers to the scale and melodic content used • 'Tal' refers to the rhythmic pattern used.
Rhythm and metre	• The piece moves from slow, rhythmically free improvisation to music with a clear pulse and energetic rhythmic patterns

	• The rhythmically free section (the alap) extends from lines 1–13
	• The jhor (lines 14–18) is marked by a more discernible pulse
	• The jhala (line 19 onwards) is distinguished by the presence of tabla
	• The tal here is based on a tintal (16-beat) rhythmic cycle, subdivided into four vibhag of four beats each
	• Increasingly florid elaborations involve:
	• Shorter note values
	• Triplets
	• 'Irregular' groupings
	• Various types of dotted rhythm.
Melody	• Draws on a rag with a flattened second and sixth
	• Has a range of three octaves
	• Includes:
	• Improvisatory elaborations of the pakad – the underlying set of pitches that is associated with the rag being used
	• Frequent use of grace notes
	• Microtonal inflections
	• Slides.
Harmony and tonality	• There is properly speaking no harmony as such, only the drone provided by the tampura
	• Tonality is non-functional in the Western sense and there is no modulation, but tonal 'gravitation' is evident in the presence of the drone and the persistent use of the rag which homes in on C (as notated in *NAM*), with many phrases ending on C
	• This rag is characterised by the augmented 2nd interval.
Structure	• *Rag Bhairav* opens with the alap, a slow improvised section introducing the pakad/melodic cells (lines 1–13)
	• The jhor is marked by a stronger sense of pulse (lines 14–18)
	• The jhala (lines 19 to the end) introduces the tabla to create a strongly marked 16-beat pulse/tintal
	• The jhala is based on the gat (i.e. an existing composition) and is typified by an accelerating pulse, a wider melodic range and shorter note lengths.
Texture and timbre	• Essentially, *Rag Bhairav* consists of a melodic line (sarangi) with drone accompaniment (tampura) and later in the music tabla providing percussion, involving contrasting timbres
	• The sympathetic strings on the sarangi result in the characteristic sound of this music.
Further listening	• Any music by the famous sitar player Ravi Shankar, e.g. the CD *Ravi in Celebration* from Angel Records.

APPLIED MUSIC 2013

Gabrieli – *Sonata pian' e forte*

Background	• The sonata was published in 1597
	• It was probably intended for performance in St Mark's Basilica, Venice on an important liturgical occasion
	• The fact that Gabrieli could call on the services of a relatively large number of instrumentalists is indicative of the wealth of the institution
	• Performance in this building would permit use of the spatially separated galleries for the two four-part groups
	• The work is historically important because it was one of the earliest to specify dynamic contrasts.
Rhythm and metre	• The sonata adopts the well-established procedure of progressing from sedate, longer note values at the start to much livelier movement towards the end
	• Time signatures have been inserted editorially. Most of the piece is notated in duple time, with occasional $\frac{3}{2}$ bars
	• Typical devices include syncopation and dotted rhythms.
Melody	• The melodic style gives the impression of a transfer of motet-like vocal writing to instruments
	• Consequently the ranges are relatively restricted
	• Much of the writing is conjunct, with the largest interval being an octave
	• 4ths and 5ths also occur relatively frequently.
Harmony	• Root-position and first-inversion chords dominate, with the occasional consonant 4th:
	• The writing is not functional but cadences are frequent, including perfect, imperfect (Phrygian) and plagal
	• Typical devices include suspensions (e.g. bar 4), circle of 5ths (e.g bars 36–41) and tierces de Picardie (e.g. bar 80).
Tonality	• The music is based on the Dorian mode on G, but cadences on most steps of the mode contribute to the work's fluid tonal scheme.
Structure	• The sonata is through-composed with clear breaks into contrasting sections

	• The only repetitions occur within sections, often in antiphony, e.g. at bar 34 where the music of bar 31 is repeated a 4th lower.
Texture	• The sonata requires two four-part instrumental groups
	• The textures include:
	• Free counterpoint for four parts (e.g. most of bars 1–13)
	• Imitation (e.g. bars 17–20)
	• Antiphony (e.g. bars 37–40)
	• Eight-part counterpoint (e.g. bars 26–31)
	• Eight-part homophony (e.g. bar 40).
Further listening	• Gabrieli – *In ecclesiis* (NAM 27)
	• Gabrieli – the CD *Music for Brass Volume 1* (Naxos 8.553609), which includes another version of *Sonata pian' e forte*.

J. S. Bach – Cantata No. 48, *Ich elender Mensch*: movements I–IV

Background	• First performed on 3 October 1723, the 19th Sunday after Trinity, in Leipzig
	• The cantata was performed before the sermon and reflected the subject matter contained in the preceding readings
	• It was intended for a small chorus and orchestra, with organ continuo
	• It is a multi-movement work which, besides chorus, recitative and aria, includes two different chorales for congregational use.
Rhythm and metre	• Movement I: triple time, with a relentless repeating pattern; includes a hemiola at bars 42–43:

	• Movement II: although notated in quadruple time, the recitative gives the impression of relatively free speech rhythms • Movement III: simple quadruple time • Movement IV: triple time ($\frac{3}{8}$), the bass line in quavers throughout, the upper parts (voice and oboe) drawing on a wider range of rhythms, e.g. the dotted rhythm of the opening phrase.

Melody	• Movement I involves a combination of:
	
	    • The ritornello motif, with rising quavers, a plunging downward leap and an appoggiatura
	
	    • The vocal lines, starting with upward leaps of usually a 5th or 6th
	
	    • The cantus firmus, based on a chorale and relatively conjunct.
	
	• Movement II is relatively angular and characterised by a number of expressive leaps:

Bar 2	Falling diminished 7th
Bars 3–4	Rising diminished 7th
Bar 10	Rising minor 7th
Bars 14–15	Rising minor 6th

	• Movement III's melody is mainly conjunct • Movement IV's melody is more instrumental in nature, with demanding leaps.
Word-setting	• Movements II and III are almost totally syllabic, except for the final phrase of the chorale • Movements I and IV involve a mixture of both syllabic and melismatic underlay.
Harmony	Bach's harmony is functional, with: • Clearly defined cadences • Tierces de Picardie (e.g. movement I bar 138) • Pedal points (e.g. movement I bars 131–138, inverted tonic pedal in oboe) • Suspensions (e.g. movement I bar 34, tenor) • Some chromatic writing (especially in movement II) • Frequent diminished 7ths.

Tonality and structure	• Movement I: ritornello, but also incorporating:
	
	    • Fugato-like choral layers
	
	    • An instrumental cantus firmus (derived from the chorale in movement VII) heard in canon in trumpet and oboe.

- The use of a cantus firmus (a pre-existing melody taken from a chorale) imposed severe limitations on the range of (entirely minor) keys that Bach could use, as the examples in the table below show:

Bar 1	G minor
Bar 43	D minor (though there is a tierce de Picardie at bar 44)
Bar 60	C minor
Bar 88	D minor

- The music returns to G minor with the concluding plagal cadence (bar 138)

- Movement II: through-composed recitative accompagnato (with orchestral accompaniment, as opposed to just continuo) with rapid modulations, moving from E♭ major to:

Bar 2	F minor
Bar 4	C minor
Bar 6	A♭ major
Bar 8	B♭ minor
Bar 9	Chromatic progressions and enharmonic change lead to…
Bar 11	E major
Bar 14	G minor
Bar 16	B♭ major

- Movement III: chorale, in B♭ major

- Movement IV: obbligato aria in ritornello form, in E♭ major:

1–16	Ritornello	E♭ major
16–38	Vocal solo	Modulates to B♭ major
39–48	Shortened ritornello	B♭ major
48–56	Vocal solo	C minor to A♭ major
56–60	Brief reference to ritornello	Starts in A♭ major
60–79	Vocal solo	F minor to E♭ major
1–16	Ritornello repeated	E♭ major

Resources and texture	• The cantata's use of resources is typically Baroque, with: • Continuo providing the harmony indicated by the figured bass • Strings • Four-part chorus • Vocal and instrumental soloists. • The vocal writing is demanding as a result of Bach's tendency to treat the voices instrumentally

	• Bach uses a wide range of textures, each movement having an individual sound
	• Movement I is the most complex, having three independent layers:
	• String ritornello (melody-dominated homophony)
	• Vocal parts (freely imitative)
	• Oboes and trumpets (chorale in canon at the 4th below).
	• Movement II: alto with homophonic strings
	• Movement III: initially homophonic setting of the chorale which then becomes contrapuntal. The orchestra doubles the voices
	• Movement IV: walking bass with oboe solo, later on counterpoint and dialogue between alto and oboe.
Further listening	• Bach – Brandenburg Concerto No. 4 in G: movement I (NAM 1)
	• Bach – Cantata No. 140, *Wachet auf!*.

Bernstein – *On the Waterfront*: 'Symphonic Suite' (opening)

Background	• This excerpt is from Bernstein's only film score
	• It was composed in 1954, and was the underscore for a film that focused on violence and corruption in the New York docks
	• The score has been criticised as film music as it tends to distract from the on-screen action.
Rhythm and metre	• Opens at an *andante* tempo in simple quadruple time
	• The tempo increases to *presto barbaro* (bar 20), with alternating duple and triple time
	• Typical devices include:
	• Ostinato
	• Syncopation
	• Off-beat accents
	• Cross-rhythmic effects.
	• The final section (bar 106) is marked *adagio* and returns to quadruple time
	• Here long, sustained notes in the strings provide a backdrop to an isolated three-note figure.
Melody	• The opening melody spans a minor 10th
	• It is arch-shaped
	• And draws on notes from the blues scale on F minor
	• Minor 3rds and diminished 5ths are prominent in the opening melody, and indeed minor 3rds play an important role throughout the extract

	• The ostinato's outline is smudged by a glissando in bars 24 and 30 • The saxophone melody at bar 42 is angular and rhythmically disjointed • From bar 70, this melody – now in oboes and violins – is fragmented.

Harmony	• Harmony is non-functional and frequently dissonant
	
	• In some passages it is difficult to hear the harmonies clearly because of the low sonorities
	
	• Typical tension-raising devices include:
	
	   • Pedals
	
	   • Tritonal clashes
	
	   • Bitonality (e.g. G minor and D major at bar 78; B major and F major from bar 106):
	
	  F major in two uppermost parts and bass
	
	  B major chord (E flat = enharmonic D sharp)

Tonality and structure	• Sections are strongly contrasted, reflecting different stages of the drama • Motivic links are created mainly through the use of minor 3rds • Tonality is non-functional, there being no cadences • The main landmarks are:

Bars	Landmark
1	Andante: opening theme in F minor (using the blues scale). Closes on F major at bar 19
20	Presto barbaro: ostinato of a minor 3rd, the basis for a layered/fugal texture. Initially in G minor, but the tonality becomes elusive with the introduction of tritones/bitonal elements
42	New theme on saxophone
54	This theme is repeated, but with shortened note lengths on woodwinds and trumpets
64	Concluding three-note figure (from bar 52) heard in simultaneous retrograde (i.e. the falling intervals of a 2nd and 6th in oboe and violin I are heard at the same time as a rising 6th and 2nd in clarinet and violin II)
78	Motif from bar 20 in tutti homophony
88	Ostinato motif and/or rhythm maintained throughout this section
106	Adagio: the three-note figure from bar 52, and its rhythm, is isolated

Resources and texture	• Large symphony orchestra with extensive percussion and solo saxophone
	• Wide range of textures and orchestral sonorities:

Bars	Landmark
1	Monophonic horn
7	Imitative flute and trombone
13	Two-part muted trumpets plus pedal
20	Percussion 'fugue'/riff plus sax melody
54	Theme in strings and woodwind in octaves
78	Tutti homophony
88	Sustained single note in violin plus side drum
106	Staggered build-up of chord, then sustained string chord with woodwind and brass stabs

Further listening	• Bernstein – the remaining parts of the 'Symphonic Suite'
	• Bernstein – 'Prologue' and 'Jet Song' from *West Side Story*.

Goldsmith – *Planet of the Apes*: 'The Hunt' (opening)

Background	• The score was composed in 1968
	• The film's futuristic content is reflected in the use of 20th-century musical techniques, e.g. the serialism evident in this excerpt
	• The alien atmosphere is conveyed by the use of additional unconventional instruments, some electronic.
Rhythm and metre	• The excerpt is characterised by driving rhythms, opening in $\frac{3}{4}$ and later involving $\frac{4}{4}$
	• There are also occasional $\frac{5}{4}$ bars
	• Typical features include:
	• Heavy stresses
	• A melody marked by long notes followed by much shorter lengths
	• Cross-rhythm of $\frac{6}{8}$ in percussion over $\frac{3}{4}$ in piano and violin II (bar 16)
	• Triplet crotchets against four quavers (bar 42)
	• Syncopation on the ram's horn (bar 52)
	• Polyrhythms (bar 56)
	• $\frac{4}{4}$ in flute and violin I superimposed with $\frac{6}{8}$ in piano and violin II (bar 84).

Melody	• Melodic lines are in general disjunct and chromatic
	• Melodic content is linked to the 12-tone motif (e.g. bars 8–9)
	• Goldsmith draws on component intervals from this line (e.g. flute in bars 13–14)
	• There is some manipulation of lines using serial methods (notice that in the examples below, the basic intervals of the row are often inverted or displaced by an octave):
	• The bass in bar 23 is a (transposed) retrograde of bars 8–9
	• The bass in bars 27–29 is a (transposed) retrograde inversion
	• The bass in bars 32–34 is a (transposed) inversion.
	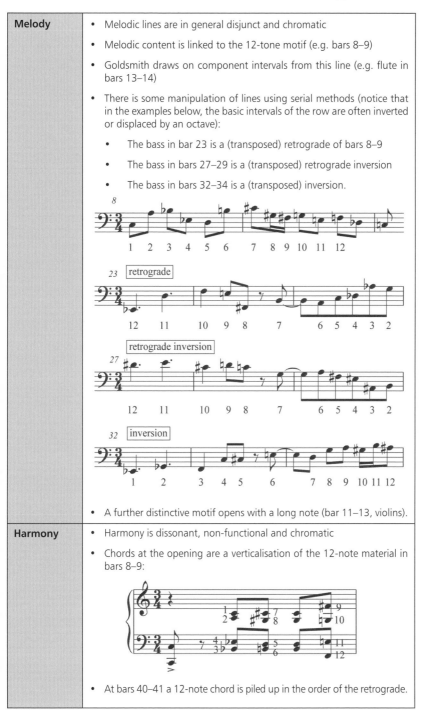
	• A further distinctive motif opens with a long note (bar 11–13, violins).
Harmony	• Harmony is dissonant, non-functional and chromatic
	• Chords at the opening are a verticalisation of the 12-note material in bars 8–9:
	• At bars 40–41 a 12-note chord is piled up in the order of the retrograde.

Tonality	Though extremely chromatic and dissonant, with polyrhythmic counterpoint often having a tonally destructive effect, there are tonal 'anchors':
	• The pounding bass Cs at the opening
	• The ostinato on G at bar 11
	• E♭ at bar 23
	• The ostinato on C at bar 45
	• A strong hint of G minor in the bass – G, B♭, A (bar 59 onwards)
	• G minor maintained in the final bars.
Structure	• The course of the music is dictated by the visual images, but the score is unified by the recurring motifs and ostinati.

Resources and textures	• Goldsmith uses a symphony orchestra, enlarged to include:
	
	  • A large percussion section, including boo bams, friction drum, vibra-slap, timbales, conga drum and bass resin drum
	
	  • Ram's horn and Tibetan horn
	
	  • Electric harp and bass clarinet.
	
	• Orchestral writing is characterised by the use of extreme ranges
	
	• Textures include:
	
	  • Homophony (e.g. bars 1–3)
	
	  • Ostinato and melody (e.g. bars 11–22)
	
	  • Polyrhythms (e.g. bars 56)
	
	  • Two-part counterpoint (e.g. bars 75–83).

Further listening	• Try viewing any other film with music by Goldsmith, e.g. *Chinatown* (1974) or *The Omen* (1976).

Gong Kebyar de Sabatu (Bali) – *Baris Melampahan*

Background	• Balinese gamelan performance requires a large ensemble of performers playing mostly tuned gongs and metallophones
	• The instruments are the property of the community rather than the individual members
	• Baris style is typical of a ritual dance performed by Balinese men to show warlike skills
	• This excerpt is in *gong kebyar* style.

Rhythm and metre	• There is a regular pulse throughout until the piece slows down at the end • Gong strokes mark the end of each rhythmic cycle (gongan) • The gongan is made up of four-beat ketegs • Throughout the extract, there is a constant 'on-beat' pulse with some 'off-beat' sounds from the reyong • Kendhang rhythms are occasionally displaced.
Melody	• The excerpt is based on a nuclear melody, built on a limited number of pitches from the pelog (selisir) scale • It is heard in varying degrees of completion • The only significant departure occurs at [H], the 'High tune'.
Harmony and tonality	• There is no harmonic progression as such • A sense of tonality results from repetitions of the pelog-derived material.
Structure	• The excerpt consists of alternations of a limited amount of musical material • Structural divisions are stressed by markers from the gong and extreme contrasts of dynamics • Sections are also clearly delineated by the addition or subtraction of forces, e.g. the angsel is marked by the addition of the reyong (gong chimes) and the kendhang (drums). • The only non-percussion instrument is the flute-like suling
Timbre, functions and texture	• The remaining instruments consist of gongs, metallophones and unpitched percussion • Gongs are deliberately pitched slightly differently to produce ombak (or acoustic 'beat') in tuning • Gongs are used to mark the end of rhythmic cycles • Metallophones provide melodic content • The texture is heterophonic.
Further listening	• The CD *Bali: Gamelan and Kecak*, recorded in Bali by David Lewiston, from Nonesuch Records.

> In this context, 'nuclear' denotes the fundamental melodic material for the entire excerpt.

INSTRUMENTAL MUSIC 2013

Debussy – *Prélude à l'après-midi d'un faune*

Background	• Debussy's work is an Impressionist piece dating from 1894
	• It is a loosely programmatic piece for orchestra, based on a poem by Mallarmé
	• This epoch-making work is regarded by Boulez as marking the start of 20th century music.
Rhythm and metre	• There is considerable flexibility in both rhythm and metre
	• The work opens in $\frac{9}{8}$, but moves freely to other compound metres ($\frac{6}{8}$ and $\frac{12}{8}$) and simple metres ($\frac{3}{4}$ and $\frac{4}{4}$)
	• The fluid rhythms make it difficult to discern the pulse because of:
	• Notes tied over barlines
	• Irregular rhythmic groupings
	• Syncopation
	• Long sustained notes
	• Application of rubato and changes of tempo.
	• Pulse is more discernible in the central passage of the work (bars 55–78)
	• Debussy also applies rhythmic augmentation (e.g. bars 79–82) and diminution (e.g. bars 83–84).
Melody	• Periodic phrasing is generally avoided
	• The work involves variation of the opening melody line rather than motivic development
	• Typical features include:
	• Chromaticism
	• Free use of tritones (e.g. bar 1):
	• Whole-tone elements (e.g. bar 36):
	• Ornamentation (chiefly acciaccaturas and trills)
	• Arabesque (flexible ornamental lines).
	• The melodies of the central passage are generally more diatonic.

Harmony and tonality	• Harmony is colouristic rather than functional • Cadences are rare • Dissonance is unprepared and unresolved (e.g. bars 4–5): • Debussy freely uses 7th, 9th, 11th and 13th chords • Parallelism occurs (e.g. bars 48–49) • Harmonic rhythm is slow.
Tonality and structure	• Tonality is frequently ambiguous because of the absence of cadences and because of the complex dissonance treatment • But key-centres are broadly discernible and help define the structure • The structure is ternary: <table><tr><td>1–54</td><td>A (subsidiary section at bar 37)</td><td>E major</td></tr><tr><td>55–78</td><td>B</td><td>D♭ major</td></tr><tr><td>79–93</td><td>A varied</td><td>E major/C major/ E♭ major/B major</td></tr><tr><td>94–110</td><td>Final statement of A</td><td>E major</td></tr></table>

Resources and texture	• Debussy used a relatively small but unusually formed orchestra
	
	• Besides strings, there are:
	
	   • Three flutes, which fulfil a major role in setting the 'tone' of the work
	
	   • Two oboes and cor anglais
	
	   • Two clarinets in A (changing to B♭ at bar 44)
	
	   • Two bassoons
	
	   • Four horns in F
	
	   • Antique cymbals (on the tonic and dominant – E and B)
	
	   • Two harps.
	
	• Stress is placed on woodwind timbres
	
	• 'Heavy' brass is not used, the only brass instruments being French horns
	
	• Strings are often played:
	
	   • Divided (*div.*)
	
	   • With mutes (*sourdines*)
	
	   • Bowed over the fingerboard (*sur la touché*)

The transposing instruments in this work are cor anglais and horns, which sound a 5th lower than written, the clarinets in A, sounding a minor 3rd lower, and the clarinets in B♭ which are a major 2nd lower.

	• Pizzicato as well as arco • Using tremolandi. • Harps play glissandi.
Further listening	• Debussy – *Nocturnes*, *La Mer* and *Images*.

Reich – *New York Counterpoint*: movement II

Background	• *New York Counterpoint* dates from 1985
	
	• It is a minimalist, post-modern work, drawing on a limited amount of thematic material
	
	• Important stylistic features are:
	
	    • Phasing (a term meaning very close imitation)
	
	    • Pulsing (meaning the rapid repetition of notes)
	
	    • Pre-recording of lines by the soloist which then form an accompaniment to a live part – other works of this type include *Vermont Counterpoint* (for flute) and *Electric Counterpoint* (for electric guitar).

Rhythm and metre	• Notated in $\frac{3}{4}$, but the pulse is difficult to discern because of the overlapping of lines • The main motif is characterised by a crotchet followed by three semiquavers, and a dislocated rhythm with interpolated rests, giving a strongly syncopated feel • The homophonic section is marked by a 'pulsing' repeated semiquaver rhythm.
Melody	• Melodic material is built entirely on a six-note/hexatonic scale • It is notated in B major without the D♯ (The only D♯s occur in the pulsing chords from bar 27) • It is constructed mainly from repetitions of a falling line • It initially spans an octave, expanding in range at bar 35 in the live clarinet part • There is some limited development arising from the derivation of new melodic lines from the underlying material (creating 'resultant melodies'), e.g. in the live clarinet part at bar 25.
Harmony and tonality	• The movement is entirely diatonic • It uses a six-note scale and is based on overlapping chords of IV and V in B major • The dissonance is partly masked by the homogeneous clarinet timbres • Harmony is essentially non-functional (lacking a drive to cadence)

	• Added-note dissonances also obscure the tonality:
	    • B major plus C♯
	    • E and G♯ plus D♯ and A♯
	    • F♯ major plus G♯.
	• The piece ends inconclusively with E and G♯.

Structure	• The structural shape of the piece is linked to the accumulation and removal of melodic strands • A contrasting section begins at bar 27 with the introduction of a 'pulsing' homophonic texture in the lowest parts • At bar 67, the texture is thinned out in a reversal of the opening procedures.
Resources and texture	• The work is written for live clarinet, performing with pre-recorded parts for eight clarinets and two bass clarinets (i.e. for a single family of instruments) • The work depends on the interweaving of melodic strands • It uses imitation, applied to two lines with the same rhythm • The imitations are very close/'phased', e.g. at the distance of a quaver in bar 3, and the distance of a quaver and crotchet in bar 13 • Pulsing homophony in four parts (bar 27) is faded in and out in pairs.
Further listening	• Reich – the remaining movements of *New York Counterpoint* • Terry Riley – *In C*.

Holborne – Pavane 'The image of melancholy' and Galliard 'Ecce quam bonum'

Background	• These pieces are examples of Elizabethan instrumental music (c. 1590s) • They feature two of the most popular dances of the time, though the complexity of the textures makes it unlikely that they were ever intended as dance music as such.
Rhythm and metre	• The Pavane has been printed in modern duple time, and draws on a range of note lengths from a semibreve down to a quaver. The longest pedal extends for six tied semibreves • The tempo is slow • The Galliard is much more lively, and is notated in $\frac{3}{2}$ • Dotted rhythms are a recurring feature • In the Galliard Holborne sometimes switches from simple triple ($\frac{3}{2}$) to compound duple ($\frac{6}{4}$) time, creating the effect of a hemiola (e.g. bar 7).

Melody	• The ranges of all parts are relatively limited
	
	• Holborne follows the conventions of the time:
	
	   • Movement is mainly conjunct
	
	   • Leaps are usually followed by compensating stepwise movement within the original interval.
	
	• Holborne also uses some inversion (e.g. bars 1–4 of the Galliard):
	
	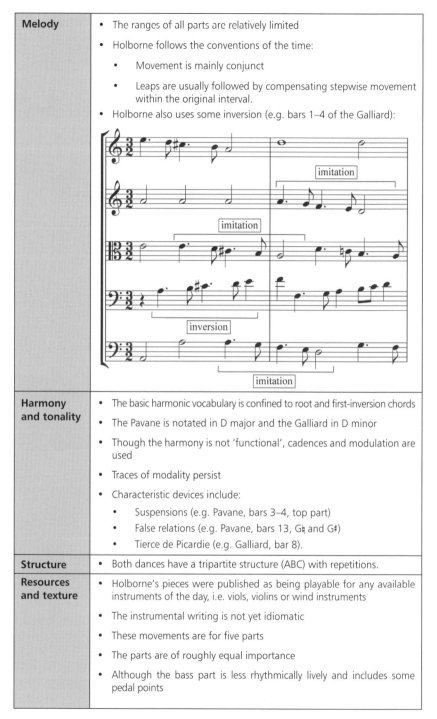

Harmony and tonality	• The basic harmonic vocabulary is confined to root and first-inversion chords
	
	• The Pavane is notated in D major and the Galliard in D minor
	
	• Though the harmony is not 'functional', cadences and modulation are used
	
	• Traces of modality persist
	
	• Characteristic devices include:
	
	   • Suspensions (e.g. Pavane, bars 3–4, top part)
	
	   • False relations (e.g. Pavane, bars 13, G♮ and G♯)
	
	   • Tierce de Picardie (e.g. Galliard, bar 8).

Structure	• Both dances have a tripartite structure (ABC) with repetitions.
Resources and texture	• Holborne's pieces were published as being playable for any available instruments of the day, i.e. viols, violins or wind instruments • The instrumental writing is not yet idiomatic • These movements are for five parts • The parts are of roughly equal importance • Although the bass part is less rhythmically lively and includes some pedal points

	• The textures are mainly contrapuntal, with imitation and occasional inversion • There is some limited use of homophony in the Galliard.
Further listening	• Sweelinck – *Pavana Lachrimae* (NAM 20).

Haydn – String Quartet in E♭, Op. 33 No. 2, 'The Joke': movement IV

Background	• The string quartet was a Classical genre developed by Haydn • This quartet was composed in 1781, and was part of a set of six that were composed 'in a new and special manner' • This excerpt is the last of the four movements • Violin I is allocated most of the melodic interest, with remaining instruments providing support • The subtitle hints at Haydn's liking for wit and humour, with many of the jokes arising from the undermining of Classical conventions (e.g. prolonged dominant pedals, and unconventionally treated second inversions) • The work was originally intended for domestic performance.
Rhythm and metre	• The time signature is compound duple ($\frac{6}{8}$), apart from the slow (Adagio) section near the end which is simple duple ($\frac{2}{4}$) • Because of the speed of the music, most note lengths are generally no shorter than a quaver • A few demisemiquavers and semiquavers occur in the Adagio • Rests play an important role, especially in setting up the jokes at the end.
Melody	• Phrasing is frequently periodic, i.e. using balanced two- and four-bar phrases, characteristic of Classical-era music • There is much stepwise (conjunct) movement with occasional larger intervals • Chromatic inflections are introduced (e.g. bar 5, B♮) • Haydn uses occasional ornaments and appoggiaturas.
Harmony	• Haydn's harmony is functional, with frequent cadences, often preceded by the supertonic chord (as in bars 7–8):

	• Other characteristic devices include:
	• Dominant pedals
	• Dissonances such as appoggiatura chords, suspensions and the dominant 9th (bar 148).
	• Second-inversion chords are left unresolved for humorous effect (e.g. bar 47).
Tonality	• The key is E♭ major, defined by cadences and pedals
	• Modulation is limited and involves A♭ major (bar 41) and F minor (bar 49) in the first episode, with occasional brief excursions to B♭ major (e.g. bar 68).
Structure	• Rondo form
	• The opening eight bars frequently recur
	• The complete structure is:

1–36	A (1–8) B (8–28) A (with repeats)
36–70	C
71–107	A B A (no repeats)
107–140	C^1 (notice the removal of D♭s to avoid modulation)
140–148	A
148–152	Adagio
152–172	A with phrases separated by rests

Resources and texture	• A single family of instruments (strings) is used conventionally (that is, bowed throughout)
	• The main texture is melody-dominated homophony
	• Variety in texture is managed through alternations of differing numbers of parts (e.g. four parts at the opening, followed by just the three upper parts)
	• Haydn also uses:
	• Pedal points of both sustained notes and articulated quavers
	• The upper two parts in 6ths
	• Double stopping (e.g. in the Adagio).
	• Dynamic and articulation indications are detailed.
Further listening	• Haydn – Symphony No. 26 in D minor: movement I (NAM 2)
	• Haydn – 'Fifths' Quartet, Op. 76 No. 2
	• Haydn – Symphony No. 104 in D.

Brahms – Piano Quintet in F minor, Op. 34: movement III

Background	• In its original form, the quintet was written for strings (1862)
	• Brahms then rewrote it for piano duet (1864)
	• The third and final form – piano quintet – dates from 1865
	• The work is intended for virtuoso players
	• This movement is the scherzo and trio, the third of the four movements
	• It is in C minor, and its conclusion prepares for the return of F minor at the start of the finale.
Rhythm and metre	• The scherzo is mainly in compound duple time ($\frac{6}{8}$), though with some switches to simple duple ($\frac{2}{4}$)
	• Typical devices include:
	• Syncopation (e.g. bars 2–4, violin I)
	• Augmentation (e.g. bars 22–25, violin I)
	• Dotted rhythms.
Melody	• The melodic lines are spun out of a limited number of motifs:
	• A rising arpeggiated line (bar 2) involving a rising sequence
	• A motif opening with repeated Gs (bar 13)
	• Part of this motif in augmentation forms the basis of the third idea, initially in C major:
	• The trio has a separate motif built partly from 3rds.
	• A further typical device is fragmentation (e.g. climax of the fugato, bars 92–100).
Harmony	• Brahms' harmony is relatively chromatic
	• There are some modal elements (e.g. the B♭ instead of B♮ in bar 19)
	• Some characteristic harmonic features are:

Bars	Harmonic feature
1	Tonic pedal
5–6	Augmented 6th not stated vertically, but implied in the individually moving parts

19	Modal dominant chord/leading note not raised
21	Dominant chord without the 3rd
22	Diatonic, initially root-position chords
26	Secondary 7ths (e.g. V^7b of VI in C major)
39	Chordal augmented 6th, resolving to V
177	Neapolitan 6th in piano, although the B♮s in the strings from bar 178 result in an inverted augmented 6th chord
180–193	Tierce de Picardie.

Tonality and structure

- The scherzo and trio as a whole is in ternary form, involving motivic development and a wide-ranging tonal scheme

- The main landmarks are as follows:

Scherzo		
Theme	Bars	Key
A	1–12	C minor
B	13–21	C minor with modal dominant
C	22–37	C major
A¹	38–45	C minor
A²	46–57	C minor to V of G minor
B¹	57–67	G minor, passing through B♭ minor at bar 64, D♭ major at bar 65, to V of E♭ minor at bar 67
Fugato	67–100	E♭ minor
B²	100–109	E♭ minor
C	109–124	E♭ major
A³	125–158	E♭/C minor
B³	158–193	C minor, closing in C major as a dominant preparation for the last movement
Trio		
D	193–225	C major, passing through G major at bar 203, B major at bar 209, a circle of 5ths at bars 213–219
E	225–241	V of C, with a dominant pedal
D¹	241–261	C major, with a brief reference to F major at bars 245–246

Resources and texture	• The quintet is scored for piano and string quartet (two violins, viola and cello)
	• Considerable demands are made on the performers:
	• Piano: dense chordal textures, a wide range, single and double octaves, broken-chord accompaniment figures, and 'percussive', attacking staccato
	• Strings: pizzicato, octaves for all four instruments, double-stopping and wide ranges.
	• Brahms uses a wide range of textures:
	• A pedal plus strings in octaves at the start
	• Brief imitations in the piano at bar 5
	• Two string instruments in octaves at bars 13–18
	• Chords plus a heterophonic line at bar 18
	• String and piano chords at bars 22–29
	• All strings in octaves with the piano in chordal imitation at bars 30–34
	• Fugato at bar 67, later on with stretto (from bar 93)
	• Piano homophony with a cello pedal at the start of the trio
	• Homophonic strings with the piano playing broken chords (from bar 210).
Further listening	• Brahms – Symphony No. 1 in C minor
	• Brahms – *Academic Festival Overture*.

Poulenc – Sonata for Horn, Trumpet and Trombone: movement I

Background	• Composed in 1922
	• Poulenc adopts a witty, irreverent, neoclassical style that shows the influence of Stravinsky
	• The first movement of a three-movement work
	• Intended for concert performance by professional performers.
Rhythm and metre	• In simple quadruple time ($\frac{4}{4}$), with occasional simple triple ($\frac{3}{4}$) bars
	• There are variations in the tempo, with a central section composed of both a slower section (*Plus lent*) and a faster one (*Plus vite*)
	• Other features include:
	• Syncopation
	• Anacrusis
	• Rhythmic displacement
	• Augmentation.

Melody	• Largely diatonic
	• Periodic phrasing reflects the Classical influences
	• Opens with a broken-chord motif in the trumpet
	• Larger leaps include 6ths and octaves, and at bar 36 there are two-octave leaps in the trumpet part
	• Major-minor fluctuations.
Harmony and tonality	• Poulenc often uses functional progressions with cadences
	• The neoclassical style is evident in the wrong-note harmony:
	• Keys are clearly defined, with modulations that help to clarify the structure.

Structure — Basically a ternary form with coda:

Section	Bars	Key
A	1–25	G major modulating to D major (bar 8)
B¹ – Plus lent	26–39	E♭ major
B² – Plus vite	40–57	B♭ major
A (incorporating part of B²)	57–85	G major
Coda	86–89	Chromaticism clouds the key, but the last two bars are in a clear G major

Resources	• The work is written for:
	• Horn in F (sounding a 5th lower than written)
	• Trumpet in C (non-transposing)
	• Trombone.
	• All parts require considerable skill in performance.
Texture	• Various forms of melody-dominated homophony
	• Limited resources enable only 'lean' harmonic support, so broken-chord patterns are used to supply this element (e.g. horn line at bar 26)

	• The accompaniment is split between trumpet and trombone at bar 40.
Further listening	• Poulenc – Concerto for Organ, Timpani and Strings in G minor • Poulenc – Gloria.

Miles Davis Quintet – *Four* (opening)

Background	• This excerpt is an example of bebop, a style of jazz that developed in the 1940s
	
	• Some typical features of bebop to be found here are:
	
	  • Extreme speed
	
	  • Virtuosity
	
	  • Dissonant harmony
	
	  • A small ensemble
	
	  • Chromaticism
	
	  • Fragmentation in the melody line
	
	  • Thematic substitution.

Rhythm and metre	• *Four* is notated in fast quadruple time, but feels more like duple time • It is persistently syncopated • Piano chords in the opening are frequently 'pushed', i.e. sounded just before the main beat • There is a rapid walking bass in crotchets.
Melody	• The melody is notated in E♭ major and played on the trumpet throughout • The opening material is based on a repeated, conjunct three-note figure • There is a mixture of conjunct and disjunct movement, with wide leaps more prominent in the later stages of the excerpt • There is much chromaticism • The range is wide, including a top F in the third chorus • There are numerous ornaments (e.g. fall-off at 1.15, pitch bend at 1.19, half-valving at 3.32) • The melody is fragmented (notice the frequent rests in the trumpet line of the first chorus).

Harmony	The main features are: • Dissonance • Chromaticism • 7th chords • Parallelism (e.g. bar H10) • Secondary dominants (e.g. C^7 in Chorus 1, bar 26) • Circle of 5ths (e.g. Chorus 1, bars 26–29) • Substitution chords (e.g. Chorus 1, bar 25, E♭ replaces Gm^7).
Tonality	• E♭ major throughout, but obscured by many of the harmonic devices listed above.
Structure	• Head arrangement (a variation structure, the 'head' being the main theme) • The head consists of bars H1–16 • It is made up of four phrases (ABAB), each lasting eight bars • It is followed by a series of variations, or 'choruses' (i.e. melodic improvisations heard over the basic chords – the changes – which are also subject to variation).

Resources and texture	• The band consists of trumpet, tenor saxophone, piano, string bass and drum kit
	
	• Demands on the instrumentalists are huge:
	
	    • Virtuoso trumpet playing and improvisation
	
	    • A wide range for the trumpet
	
	    • Ornamentation (e.g. split notes, fall offs, pitch bends, ghost notes, quarter tones, half-valving)
	
	    • Rhythmic complexity
	
	    • A fast tempo.
	
	• The texture is mainly melody-dominated homophony
	
	• The sax doubles the trumpet an octave lower in the head
	
	• The piano comps
	
	• The bass plays a pizzicato walking bass.

Further listening	• Miles Davis – the CD *Milestones* • Dizzy Gillespie – *Manteca* and *A Night in Tunisia*.

> Comping simply refers to the playing of chords.

APPLIED MUSIC 2014

Wagner – Prelude to *Tristan und Isolde*

Background	• The Prelude was first performed in 1859, but the complete opera was only staged for the first time in 1865
	• The libretto was written by Wagner himself, and drew on medieval sources
	• In Wagner's treatment, the lovers' passions are requited only in death
	• The work is of major significance, opening new avenues that led directly to late romanticism and the atonality of early 20th-century music
	• The Prelude paves the way for the atmosphere and content of the opera itself (Act I of which follows without a break), moving from insatiable longing to rapture, then back to a state of languor
	• Wagner used German-language musical directions. Translations are given at the end of the Anthology.
Rhythm and metre	• The Prelude is in slow compound duple ($\frac{6}{8}$) time
	• The pulse is not always easy to discern because of pauses, silences and notes tied over barlines
	• As the music moves towards the main climax, note values become shorter
	• Dotted rhythms frequently occur.

Melody	• The 'un-ending melody' is woven from a series of leitmotifs:
	
	    • Grief and Desire motifs:
	
	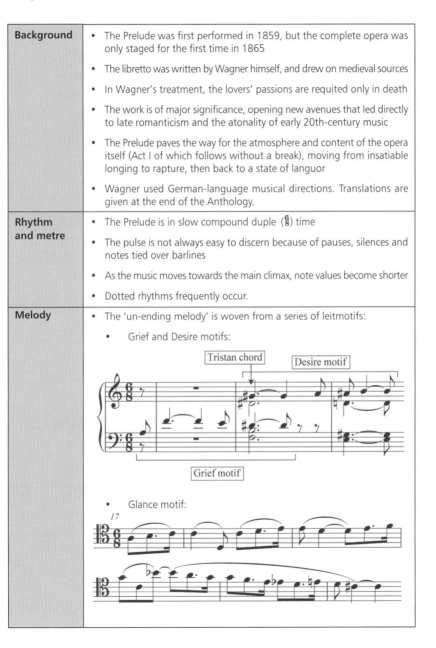
	
	    • Glance motif:

	• Love-potion motif:
	
	• Characteristic aspects are:
	
	   • Chromaticism
	
	   • Appoggiaturas
	
	   • 'Yearning' rising minor 6th in the Grief motif
	
	   • Falling 7th/dotted-rhythm figure in the Glance and Love-potion motifs
	
	   • Sequential repetition
	
	   • Inversion
	
	   • Fragmentation.

Harmony	• Wagner's harmony is functional, but notable for reinforcing the mood of longing by avoiding closure
	
	• Therefore there are few perfect cadences but some notable interrupted cadences (e.g. bars 16–17)
	
	• Characteristic devices include:
	
	   • 'Tristan' chord (formed from an augmented 6th plus an appoggiatura)
	
	   • Unresolved dominant 7th chords
	
	   • Diminished 7th
	
	   • Neapolitan 6th
	
	   • Dominant pedal (to increase tension).

Tonality and structure	• The sense of key is weakened through chromaticism, unresolved dissonance and the avoidance of perfect cadences • The structure can be described as follows: <table><tr><td>Bars</td><td>Theme / keys</td></tr><tr><td>1–24</td><td>Exposition</td></tr><tr><td>1–17</td><td>Theme 1, passing through:</td></tr><tr><td>1</td><td>A minor</td></tr><tr><td>4–7</td><td>C major</td></tr><tr><td>8–11</td><td>E minor</td></tr><tr><td>16</td><td>A minor</td></tr></table>

17–24	Theme 2 (Glance), passing through:
21	D minor
23	B major
24–65	Middle section in ternary form beginning with Theme 3 (Love-potion), passing through:
25	A major
29	E minor
36	D minor
43–44	(Interrupted cadence in) C♯ minor
45	E major
63	Dominant pedal in A major
66–83	First recapitulation: climactic presentation mainly of opening motifs. Ambiguous tonality, but moving from A to E♭ minor.
84–111	Second recapitulation: a 'thinned-out' presentation of the opening motifs and Glance motif. Tonality moves from A minor to C minor.
106	C minor, dominant preparation for opening of Act 1

Resources and texture	• The Prelude is scored for a large orchestra, including the following transposing instruments:
	• Cor anglais, sounding a perfect 5th below the printed pitch
	• Clarinets in A, sounding a minor 3rd below the printed pitch
	• Bass clarinet, also sounding a minor 3rd below the printed pitch
	• Two horns in F, sounding a perfect 5th below the printed pitch
	• Two horns in E, sounding a minor 6th below the printed pitch
	• Two trumpets in F, sounding a perfect 4th above the printed pitch
	• Double basses, which sound an octave lower than written.
	• Some technical devices used by Wagner in the string writing include:
	• Tremolo
	• Sul G (playing on the G string for its particular timbre)
	• Pizzicato
	• Divisi (in German, *geteilt*).
	• Wagner's diversity of orchestral textures is evident in the following features:
	• Melody-dominated homophony (as in the opening)

	• Antiphonal exchange between different instruments (bars 10–15)
	• Orchestral polyphony, arising from combinations of leitmotifs (e.g. bars 80–82)
	• Pedal points
	• Low octaves (at the end).
Further listening	• Wagner – 'Liebestod' from *Tristan und Isolde* (the concluding passage of the opera)
	• Wagner – *Wesendonck Lieder* (in which Wagner used some of the motifs to be found in *Tristan und Isolde*).

Taverner – *O Wilhelme, pastor bone*

Background	• *O Wilhelme* is an antiphon, composed around 1528
	• The antiphon is a choral work similar to an anthem or motet with Latin text, usually in the nature of a prayer
	• *O Wilhelme* was sung at Compline, the last service of the day, at Cardinal College (now Christ Church) in Oxford, where Taverner was Master of the Choristers
	• The work includes a reference to Cardinal Wolsey, the founder of the college.
Rhythm and metre	• The work is printed in modern notation with the time signature of $\frac{4}{4}$ inserted
	• There is one bar written in $\frac{3}{2}$ (bar 31)
	• Note lengths range from semibreves to quavers, with occasional dotted rhythms. The predominance of crotchets and minims is a hallmark of the 'plain' style of this period.
Melody and word-setting	• The range of each part is relatively narrow (between a 9th and 11th)
	• The melody lines draw mainly on the major scale (or Ionian mode), although there are occasional chromatic alterations
	• Leaps are usually followed by stepwise movement in the opposite direction
	• Lines are mostly conjunct
	• Lengths of phrases are dictated by the text, and therefore irregular
	• Word setting is mainly syllabic
	• But the passage at bar 61 is melismatic (a conventional treatment of the penultimate syllable of a phrase).
Harmony	• The harmonic vocabulary consists of root and first-inversion chords
	• There is little on-beat dissonance

	• Though the 6–5 line in the countertenor part in the last bar involves resolution of an unstable harmonic structure
	
	• Other devices include:
	    • False relations (bars 40–41, 50–51)
	    • Passing notes (e.g. bar 50)
	    • Cambiata (bar 52).

Tonality and structure	• *O Wilhelme* is essentially modal, with occasional chromatic inflections • It seems to be in F (Ionian mode) • There are central sections in G minor with tierces de Picardie • There is a plagal cadence at the end • The work is through-composed • And in two main sections (reflecting the structure of the text): bars 1–32 and 33–end.

Texture	• The antiphon was written for five parts
	
	• Taverner uses a range of textures and voice combinations:
	    • Antiphony
	    • Free counterpoint
	    • Imitative counterpoint
	    • Homorhythm
	    • Gymel (the temporary splitting of a line into two parts).

Further listening	• Taverner – *Missa Gloria Tibi Trinitas*.

Haydn – 'Quoniam tu solus' from *The Nelson Mass*

Background	• *The Nelson Mass* was originally entitled *Missa in Angustiis* ('Mass in the time of fear') • It was one of a series of six masses composed to celebrate the Name Day of the Princess Esterházy, Haydn being in the service of this family • It dates from August 1798, and was first performed that year • Nelson's name is associated with the work as he is thought to have heard it when he travelled through Austria in 1800 • 'Quoniam tu solus' is the final section from the Gloria.
Rhythm and metre	• In Allegro $\frac{4}{4}$ throughout

	• The work is characterised by jaunty dotted rhythms, fast-moving scalic figures and occasional syncopation.
Melody and word-setting	• Some periodic phrasing (e.g. bars 1–2 are answered by 3–4) • Repetition of phrases • Lines composed from combinations of stepwise movement and broken-chord figures • Word-setting is mainly syllabic, though the Amens are generally melismatic (e.g. bars 68–70).
Harmony	• Functional harmony • Frequent cadences • Pedal points (e.g. bars 61–68).

Tonality and structure	• Tonality is established by functional harmonic progressions with cadences and modulations to related keys
	
	• The structure involves the co-ordination of various elements:
	
	   • Bars 1–22: free-formed, but built on generally balanced phrases
	
	   • Anchored to D major, with a tonic pedal (bars 15–21) shifting to the dominant chord at the end
	
	   • Bars 22–61: fugato
	
	   • Modulates here to: B minor (bar 32); A major (bar 37); E minor (bar 44); G major (bar 49); dominant pedal in D (bar 54)
	
	   • Bars 61–82: coda (canonic elements with solo voices)
	
	   • Anchored to D major by tonic pedal points; lack of modulation; repeated perfect cadences.

Resources and texture	• The opulence of the resources indicates that the mass was originally intended for performance in only the most richly endowed institutions
	
	• It requires:
	
	   • Four solo voices (SATB)
	
	   • SATB chorus
	
	   • Orchestra of strings, three trumpets (clarini), timpani and organ.
	
	• The movement opens with a melody-dominated texture
	
	• The solo soprano is answered (antiphonally) by homophonic four-part chorus
	
	• The orchestral parts are independent, but with some heterophony
	
	• Other features here include pedals and orchestral scales
	
	• From bar 22 there is a fugato with:
	
	   • Subject in the bass (bar 22)
	
	   • Answer in the tenor (bar 24)

	• Counter-subject in e.g. the bass (bar 24)
	• Second counter-subject in e.g. the bass (bar 26)
	• Stretto, e.g. where the soprano enters in bar 47.
	• In the fugato the orchestra doubles the voice parts
	• From bar 61 there are canonic entries in the solo voices, with a pedal and broken chords in the orchestra
	• There is free counterpoint in the chorus at bar 77
	• And homophony in the chorus at bar 80.
Further listening	• Haydn – *The Creation*, in particular the chorus 'The Heavens Are Telling'.

James Horner – *Titanic*: 'Take her to sea, Mr Murdoch'

Background	• Composed in 1997 for an epic blockbuster film about the sinking of the Titanic ship
	• Horner was born in Los Angeles but studied at the Royal College of Music in London
	• The score reflects some British influences, e.g. the use of folk song and modality are reminiscent of Vaughan Williams.
Rhythm and metre	• The score moves flexibly from one metre to another ($\frac{3}{4}$, $\frac{4}{4}$, $\frac{3}{2}$, $\frac{5}{4}$, etc.), and also through changing tempi as the action proceeds
	• Striking effects include:
	• Repeated semiquaver and quaver rhythms (bar 21)
	• A $\frac{5}{4}$ dance rhythm (bar 37)
	• Rhythmic augmentation of the opening theme (bar 106).
Melody	• Melodic lines are frequently based on scalic motifs
	• There is some modality (e.g. Lydian at the opening)
	• There is use of folk-derived material at bar 30.
Harmony and tonality	• The music is tonal, though there is an avoidance of cadences
	• There are numerous tertiary relationships (e.g. from the opening in E♭, the music moves to G at bar 8 then to B at bar 15)
	• Other tonal areas include:
	• G at bar 30
	• D at bar 57
	• B at bar 86.

	• Characteristic devices include:
	
	    • Dominant and tonic pedals
	
	    • Lydian inflections
	
	    • A chord without a 3rd at the end.

Structure	• The score is through-composed, the course of the music being dictated by images on screen • Underlying unity is achieved through the use of recurring themes and motifs.
Resources and texture	• The work requires a symphony orchestra including tubular bells, bell tree, sleigh bells, synthesiser (voices and organ) and wordless choir • Textures used include:

Bars	Texture
1	Pedal and imitation in voices, viola, violins, bassoons and clarinets
4	Homophony
8	Broken chords in violins and harps
15	Layered, with simultaneous ostinati, one of rising and falling octaves in cellos, piano and bassoons, another of rising and falling scales in violins, horns and clarinets
23	Homophonic (almost tutti)
30	Pedal plus two vocal upper parts, doubled in woodwind; tremolo in strings
37	Homophony for strings and synthesiser
57	Horn countermelody
68	Pedal of reiterated notes

Further listening	• Try viewing another of the films for which Horner wrote incidental music, e.g. *Braveheart* (1995) or *The Mask of Zorro* (1998).

Red Stripe Ebony Steelband (Trinidad) – *Yellow Bird*

Background	• An instrumental arrangement of a calypso – a type of Afro-Caribbean song, often with satirical content • Traditionally performed in Trinidad during the Carnival period.
Rhythm and metre	• Notated in quadruple metre, though rapid enough to feel like duple time • There is a persistent ♩. ♪ ♩ ♩ tango rhythm in the bassline • Syncopations are frequent in the upper parts.

Melody	• The melody is fundamentally diatonic
	• There is minimal chromaticism
	• The melody spans a major 9th
	• It consists of mainly four-bar phrases, except for one phrase of five bars (bars 21–25)
	• There is some use of sequence
	• There are varied repetitions
	• And prominent triadic lines.
Harmony and tonality	• Diatonic, with persistent perfect cadences
	• Harmonies are restricted to primary triads
	• The key is G major with no modulation.

Structure		

Bars	Theme
1–16	A repeated
17–25	B
26–41	A repeated
42–51	B

Resources and texture	• Performed on a family of percussion instruments (steel pans) fashioned from oil drums
	• Accompanied by drum-kit
	• The texture is essentially rhythmically-enlivened melody-dominated homophony
	• A brief countermelody appears at bar 28
	• Tremolo is used to produce the longer note lengths.

INSTRUMENTAL MUSIC 2014

J. S. Bach – Brandenburg Concerto No. 4 in G: movement I

Background	• One of six concertos written between 1717 and 1722
	• The excerpt in NAM is the first of the three movements that make up this work
	• Bach was strongly influenced by Vivaldi in his approach to the concerto grosso

Rhythm and metre	• Allegro $\frac{3}{8}$ • Syncopation • Hemiola (e.g. bars 80–81).
Melody	*Fortspinnung* technique is applied to: • Broken-chord patterns • Scalic material.

Harmony	• Functional and mainly diatonic
	
	• The harmonic vocabulary consists of:
	
	   • Chords in root position and all inversions
	
	   • Dominant 7ths
	
	   • Neapolitan 6th when the music moves to a minor key:
	
	   • Frequent harmonic sequences
	
	   • Circle of 5ths
	
	   • Pedal points
	
	   • Suspensions.
	
	• There is a varied harmonic rhythm, which often speeds up towards cadences and slows down in the solos.

Structure and tonality	• Ritornello form • Modulations mark the different stages of the structure

> *Fortspinnung* is the spinning out of material from the main motif, involving repetition, sequence, inversion, and various rhythmic and melodic elaborations.

- The main sections are as follows:

Bars	Theme	Key
1–83	Ritornello	G major
83–137	Episode	Modulates to D major at bar 103
137–157	Shortened ritornello	E minor
157–209	Episode	Includes a reference to the ritornello opening in A minor (bar 185)
209–235	Ritornello	C major
235–323	Episode	Closes in B minor
323–345	Shortened ritornello	B minor
345–427	Complete ritornello	G major

- The middle ritornelli always end with the equivalent of the last 15 bars of the opening ritornello.

Resources and texture	• Typical concerto grosso textural layout, with a concertino of two recorders and solo violin, plus a strings ripieno section with harpsichord continuo
	
	• Typical textures include:
	
	   • Melody-dominated homophony
	
	   • Trio sonata-style passages
	
	   • Brief snatches of imitation/canon.
	
	• The violin has the most demanding solo part, with:
	
	   • A wide range, from open-string G to the G three octaves above
	
	   • The use of fifth position
	
	   • A rapid demisemiquaver passage from bar 187
	
	   • Double- and triple-stopping.

Further listening	• Bach – any of the other Brandenburg Concerti.

Webern – Quartet Op. 22: movement I

Background	• This work dates from 1930, and is an example of serialism • Serialism was a compositional technique associated with the Second Viennese School, in particular Schoenberg and Berg as well as Webern • Schoenberg was regarded as the leader of the group, and Webern was one of his students

	• Webern's music tends to be very compressed, resulting in short, concentrated works
	• It also shows signs of neoclassicism in its reliance on counterpoint and symmetrical structure
	• This work was intended for concert performance by professional musicians.
Rhythm and metre	• The movement is mainly in $\frac{3}{8}$, but with frequent changes to $\frac{4}{8}$ and $\frac{5}{8}$
	• From bar 24 to the end, it is all in $\frac{3}{8}$
	• However, the pulse is difficult to detect because of 'pointilliste' instrumentation and offbeat placing of material within the bars
	• The work is built almost completely on three rhythmic cells:
	(i) (ii) (iii)
	• The most notable exception is the set of four semiquavers at bars 12–13
	• Rests contribute to the effect of rhythmic dislocation.
Melody	• Melodic lines are angular, i.e. they are marked by large leaps
	• Typical large intervals include:
	• Major 7th/diminished octave
	• Minor 9th
	• Major 10th.
	• Octave displacements are frequent (compare the saxophone melody at bars 6–10 with its recapitulation across the violin, clarinet and saxophone at bar 28)
	• All melodic material derives from the row (see below under Tonality).
Harmony	• There is a total absence of conventional harmonic procedures such as cadences
	• Vertical structures frequently consist of no more than two notes
	• The music is dissonant, with no preparation or resolution.
Tonality	• The work is atonal
	• It is a serial work based on a 12-note row; that is, all 12 notes of a chromatic scale are heard in a fixed order
	• The basic note-order – the 'prime order' – is heard in the tenor saxophone part in bars 6–10

	• This order is used throughout, sometimes in:
	• Transposed form, that is beginning on any note, e.g. the violin in bar 2 starts the prime order ten semitones higher than the prime in bar 6
	• Inversion (the intervals of the prime are presented 'upside down', e.g. compare the tenor saxophone in bars 1–2 with the first three notes of the prime in bars 6–7)
	• Retrograde (the intervals of the prime are presented in reverse order, e.g. compare the piano right-hand part in bar 21 with the saxophone part of bar 10)
	• Retrograde-inversion (the intervals are presented both upside down and running backwards, e.g. compare the saxophone part of bar 24 with the saxophone part of bar 10).

Structure	• The structure of the work is clearly defined
	
	• It can be regarded as being in ternary/ rounded binary or sonata form, with:
	    • An introduction (bars 1–5)
	    • The first repeated section, which is a sort of exposition, with the prime clearly announced in the saxophone
	    • The second repeated section, which contains the equivalent of a development and from bar 28 a recapitulation
	    • A coda (bars 40–43), which presents the introductory material in retrograde.
	
	The note-rows are particularly difficult to follow in this work because of the way Webern splits the notes between the various instruments. E.g. the transposed prime order in the opening bars passes from the violin to the piano, violin, clarinet and finishes in the left-hand piano part. The situation becomes still more complicated as the inverted row is heard simultaneously in the saxophone.

Resources and texture	• There is an unusual selection and combination of performing forces in this work (compare with the Haydn string quartet)
	
	• A wide range of performance techniques is used:
	    • Pizzicato/arco (violin)
	    • Mute on and off (violin)
	    • Rapid contrasts of articulation and dynamics (all instruments)
	    • Spread chords in both directions (piano).
	
	• Webern frequently uses isolated notes or points of sound (a technique known as 'pointillism')
	
	• He also uses *Klangfarbenmelodie* (sound-colour-melody), with the melody line split between different instruments. E.g. compare the original statement of the prime in bars 6–10, which is entirely on the tenor saxophone, with its restatement starting at bar 28:
	    • Bar 28: clarinet C♯–E
	    • Bars 29–30: violin F–D; clarinet D♯–B

	• Bars 30–31: tenor sax B♭ A G♯
	• Bar 32: violin F♯–C–G.
	• The texture can be described as contrapuntal with mirror canons (e.g. compare the saxophone line of bars 1–2 with the violin in bar 2, which imitates the saxophone but in inversion)
	• The texture intensifies at the climax in the development, with more overlapping of parts.
Further listening	• Berg – Violin Concerto.

Beethoven – Septet in E♭, Op. 20: movement I

Background	• Composed in 1799 and first performed in 1800
	• One of Beethoven's most conventionally Classical works
	• The first movement of a six-movement work
	• The relatively large number of movements and the size of the ensemble indicate links with the serenade type of Classical music
	• The size of the ensemble also makes it suitable for concert as much as chamber performance.
Rhythm and metre	• Opens with a slow (Adagio) triple time (¾) section, including demisemiquaver passages
	• Followed by fast (Allegro con brio) duple time (𝄵)
	• Rhythmic features include:
	• Anacrusis
	• Syncopation
	• Triplets
	• Diminution in the closing bars.
Melody	• The melody in the Adagio features a combination of broken chords and conjunct movement, and ornamentation (acciaccaturas and a trill)
	• In the Allegro con brio, the opening motif of the first subject (three quavers) is derived from a similar figure in the Adagio (see bar 8, violin)
	• Other features include:
	• Sequence
	• Periodic (balanced) phrasing
	• Ornamentation (trills, acciaccaturas, turns)
	• Chromaticism
	• Scalic patterns.

Harmony	• Functional, with frequent cadences, both imperfect and perfect
	• Chords appear in root position and all inversions
	• The harmonic rhythm (rate of chord change) increases as cadences are approached
	• Pedal points are used to raise tension
	• There is some chromatic harmony, for example the German (augmented) 6th at bar 7.
Tonality	• The movement is in E♭ major, with modulations
	• Key changes are closely related to the underlying structure:
	• The second subject appears in the dominant
	• The development includes passages in C minor, A♭ major and F minor
	• The second subject in the recapitulation remains in E♭ major.
	• Beethoven also touches on the tonic minor (E♭ minor) in the introduction.
Structure	• A slow introduction followed by sonata form
	• The main sections are:

Bars	Section
	Exposition
18	First subject
40	Transition
53	Second subject
98	Codetta
111	Development
	Recapitulation
154	First subject
188	Second subject
233	Coda

Forces and texture	• Scored for three wind instruments and four strings, including double bass
	• Notice the use of transposing instruments:
	• Clarinet in B♭ sounds a major 2nd below the printed pitch
	• Horn in E♭ sounds a major 6th below the printed pitch.
	• Beethoven uses multiple stops in the violin and viola for additional force
	• He uses many different types of texture, and constantly varies the number of instruments involved
	• The Adagio opens with a contrast between tutti chords and a single (monophonic) violin line

	• At bar 8, three-part string chords are heard in alternation with tutti chords
	• At the opening of the Allegro con brio, Beethoven uses melody-dominated homophony for three instruments, followed by an expanded melody-dominated homophony for all instruments
	• Other textural features include:
	• Antiphony (or dialogue) at bars 47–49
	• Melody in octaves (bars 111–115)
	• Homorhythm (bars 53–55)
	• Pedal (bars 140–153)
	• Imitation (bars 258–264).
Further listening	• Beethoven – Symphony No. 1 • Schubert – Octet.

Sweelinck – *Pavana Lachrimae*

See pages 33–35.

Schumann – *Kinderscenen*, Op. 15: Nos. 1, 3 and 11

Background	• Three short pieces from a set of 13 miniatures
	• Sometimes described as 'character' pieces, intended to convey emotional states or moods, and so programmatic to some degree (compare with Berlioz's *Harold in Italy*).
Rhythm and metre	All three are in simple duple time (²⁄₄), but:
	• No. 1 has constant triplet quavers in the accompaniment
	• No. 3 has running semiquavers
	• No. 11 changes tempo, and contains off-beat chords and dotted rhythms.
Melody	• All pieces are characterised by periodic/balanced phrasing and sequence
	• No. 1 is typified by a rising minor 6th at the start of many of the phrases:

	• No. 3 is frequently conjunct
	• No. 11 contains a variety of motifs, some quite wide in range (e.g. bass line bars 9–12). There is also chromaticism.
Harmony	• Functional
	• Particular features are as follows:
	• No. 1 contains diminished 7ths and a circle of 5ths in bars 9–12
	• No. 3 uses a double pedal on C and G at bars 13–14, resulting in a 'Neapolitan' inflection (that is, a chord on the flattened supertonic)
	• No. 11 uses various cadences, including the interrupted (bar 26).
Tonality	Limited or no modulation:
	• No. 1 is in G major throughout
	• No. 3 is in B minor throughout
	• No. 11 is in G major, but touches on E minor and C major. Chromaticism sometimes makes statements of the key less clear.
Structure	• No. 1: rounded binary with repeats
	• No. 3: rounded binary with repeats
	• No. 11: simple rondo.
Texture	• Melody-dominated homophony with idiomatic piano-writing and use of the sustaining pedal
	• No. 3 uses a sort of 'stride' bass
	• No. 11 is notable for shifting the melody from the right to left hand, and for off-beat accents.
Further listening	• Schumann – *Carnaval*.

Debussy – *Pour le piano*: 'Sarabande'

Background	• The Sarabande was composed in 1894 and reflects Debussy's interest in earlier musical forms
	• It is the second of the three movements that make up *Pour le piano*
	• The piano writing is not yet Impressionistic.
Rhythm and metre	• The movement is in slow triple time, typical of the sarabande
	• The characteristic emphasis on the second beat is evident in the placing of minims in e.g. bars 2, 4 and 14
	• Other features include streams of quavers and the hemiola-like cross rhythm at bars 67–68.

Melody	• Phrases are generally balanced (e.g. bars 1 2 and 3 4) • The melody is formed from a combination of stepwise movement and relatively small leaps • There are frequent immediate repetitions, sometimes with slight variations (e.g. bars 23–24 and 25–26) • The melody has a relatively restricted range, though it is slightly broader at the end of the piece.
Harmony	Characteristic features include: • Modal cadences (e.g. chords I–VII at bars 7–8) • Parallel 7ths (e.g. bars 11–12 in the bass stave) • Half-diminished chords (e.g. bar 1 beat 1) • Quartal harmony, i.e. chords made up of superimposed 4ths (e.g. bars 23–29) • Parallel added-6th chords (e.g. bars 35–41) • 9th and 13th chords (e.g. bar 50 beat 1 and bar 30 beat 2 respectively) • Common chords (e.g. bar 56) • Chords without a 3rd (e.g. bar 63) • Changing harmonisation of a recurring melody (e.g. compare bar 42 with bar 1).
Tonality	• The Sarabande is predominantly in the Aeolian mode transposed to C♯ • The use of modal harmony leads to unusual cadences (e.g. chords I–VII at bars 7–8) • Other devices cloud the tonality, e.g whole-tone movement in the bass and quartal harmony (based on 4ths)
Structure	• Ternary or rondo:

Bars	Theme	Comments
1–8	A	Bars 1–2 are repeated (with variation) in 3–4
9–14	B	Ends with a cadence on chord II (major)
15–22	A¹	Ends in C♯ minor with an implied plagal cadence
23–41	C	Bars 25–26 are a modified repetition of 23–24; bar 27 is a transposed repetition of 23; bar 33 is a transposed repetition of 29
42–49	A²	Changed harmonisation of opening bars
50–55	D	New material
56–62	B¹	First 4 bars transposed, bar 60 returns to C♯ minor
63–72		Coda

Texture	<ul><li>Debussy uses the full range of the piano and requires constant use of the sustaining pedal.</li><li>Textures are mainly homophonic:</li></ul>

Bars	Texture
1	Six-part homophony
5	Octaves
9	Melody with an independent chordal accompaniment
11	Parallel 7th chords
20	Octaves in a very low register
23	Parallel 4th chords (quartal harmony)
29	Right-hand octaves supported by chords
35	Parallel 6th and inverted 7th chords
56	Melody supported by parallel common chords

Further listening	<ul><li>Debussy – *Suite Bergamasque*</li><li>For an Impressionistic work, listen to *Reflets dans l'eau* from *Images I*.</li></ul>

Duke Ellington and his Orchestra – *Black and Tan Fantasy*

Background	<ul><li>*Black and Tan Fantasy* was first recorded in 1927</li><li>Ellington was then working at the Cotton Club in New York</li><li>The title refers to the mixed-race nightclubs known as 'black and tan' clubs.</li><li>The work is in quadruple 'steady swing' time</li></ul>
Rhythm and metre	<ul><li>Quavers are therefore uneven</li><li>Other features include:<ul><li>A regular crotchet rhythm (bars 1–12)</li><li>A 'pad'/sustained chord from bar 13 with every other beat sounded in the bass, supporting a melody that combines duplet and triplet quavers. These are often tied across the beat with some cross-phrasing/rhythm at bar 17</li><li>Triplet crotchets at bar 33</li><li>Syncopation (e.g. bar 41)</li><li>Semiquavers at bar 61</li><li>Dotted rhythms at bar 87</li><li>The pulse slackens at the end.</li></ul></li></ul>

Melody	• Pre-existing melodic material is derived from the popular song *The Holy City*, and Chopin's 'Funeral March' from Piano Sonata No. 2
	• Improvised material covers a wide range.
Harmony	• The harmony is built on a 12-bar blues progression
	• It is varied by the use of substitution chords
	• 7th/9th chords are regularly used (e.g. diminished 7th at bar 58)
	• There is a circle of 5ths (bars 59–63)
	• There are varying rates of harmonic change
	• The work ends with a plagal cadence.
Structure and tonality	• The structure is a head arrangement, consisting of:
	• A 12-bar blues with varied repeats
	• A 16-bar interruption at bar 13
	• A four-bar coda, quoting Chopin's 'Funeral March' (bar 87).
	• The piece starts in B♭ minor, changing to B♭ major for the central section that begins at bar 13
	• It returns to B♭ minor at the end, reinforced by a plagal cadence.
Resources and texture	• *Black and Tan Fantasy* requires a large group of players, involving 'reeds' (saxophones and clarinet), 'brass' (trumpet and trombone) and the 'rhythm' section (piano, banjo, drums and bass)
	• Special effects are used, associated with the 'jungle' style, e.g. growls and a horse whinny
	• Textures are predominantly homophonic
	• Specific features include:

Bars 1–12	Melody with a second supporting part, often in 6ths
Bars 13–28	Saxophone solo with more sustained supporting harmonies
Bars 29–86	Series of 12-bar improvised variations, typically with melody-dominated homophony, with one variation for piano at bars 53–64 involving stride bass
Bars 87–90	Tutti homophonic

| **Further listening** | • Duke Ellington – *The Mooche, Mood Indigo* and *Creole Rhapsody.* |

Sample questions for Sections B and C

Below are examples of the types of question normally set in these sections of the paper. Read through them carefully so that you are sure about the sort of information you are required to provide. If you are uncertain about what is meant, refer to the glossary at the end of this book.

You will notice that the examiner's commentary refers to basic points and illustrated points. A mark is awarded for a basic point without further elaboration. For example, in an essay on harmony in Holborne's pavane, a comment to the effect that Holborne uses cadences would gain a mark for a basic point. If, however, the candidate had added that there was a perfect cadence in bars 14–15, the observation about cadences would then count as an illustrated point. Very often the illustration will take the form of a location, but there may also be occasions when other types of amplification are possible. For example, in an essay on Goldsmith's score for *Planet of the Apes*, a candidate would receive a basic mark for saying that Goldsmith uses a large symphony orchestra with some unusual instruments, but an illustrated mark would be given for adding a comment about the use of ram's horn, electric harp and the like.

APPLIED MUSIC 2012 (SECTION B)

SAMPLE QUESTION 1

Diaghilev asked Stravinsky for arrangements of various 18th-century works for the ballet score of *Pulcinella*. Focusing on harmony and texture in 'Gavotta con due variazioni' (NAM 7), offer reasons for Diaghilev's initial shocked reaction to the result. (13)

Before studying the mark scheme (indicative content) that follows, attempt the question yourself. Notice that the key words are *harmony*, *texture*, *'Gavotta con due variazioni'* and *shocked reaction*. You may find it convenient to refer briefly to the historical context, but take care to keep your remarks relevant. Do not waste time on any aspect of the Gavotta that is not related to harmony and texture.

Indicative content	
Harmony	• Functional framework (derived from the original works) with perfect cadences. Original works are modified by addition of pedals and horn appoggiaturas.
	Other noteworthy features:
	• Bar 43: tonic chord clashes with subdominant chord
	• Bar 51: unprepared dissonance in oboe 2 line
	• Bar 69: modulation to A major weakened by ambiguous G♮ in bassoon 1
	• Bar 76: unprepared dissonance in flute

	• Bar 79: oboe 1 has new countermelody creating suspensions
	• Bars 80 and 83: weakened perfect cadences, with partial resolution and changes of register.
Texture	• Scored for wind and brass instruments only. Instrumentation aimed at producing typical neoclassical, non-expressive, anti-Romantic sound.
	• The original basic two-part texture is expanded by addition of countermelodies (e.g. horn in bar 39, oboe 2 at bar 50).
	Other features:
	• Additional accompaniment figuration; sustained notes; glissandi in bassoon; Alberti bass in bassoon; rapid runs in the two flutes.

Examiners arrive at a final mark for these questions using a holistic grid. For full details see Edexcel's *Sample Assessment Materials*. For the present, it is enough to know that the full 13 marks will be awarded to work that contains at least nine relevant, well-illustrated points, showing excellent organisation and planning, and expressed coherently without significant spelling or grammatical errors.

As you work through this section of the book, and see examples of work of different standards, you will see how the holistic grid is applied across the available mark range.

Sample answer 1

> Harmony in the *Gavotta* is basically traditional, as is the form which is binary. The first section, up to the repeat sign at bar 10, starts in D and as expected moves to A major, and the second section modulates more widely. There is a section in G to begin with, then a sequential repeat in A, then a series of cadences in F♯ minor, E minor and D. The variations all follow the same pattern.
>
> Cadences also follow traditional 'functional' patterns [1] with e.g. imperfect cadences in bars 4 and 10 [x].
>
> There are also many examples of 'wrong-note' harmony which was typical of the neoclassical style developed in the 1920s [1]. There is a glaring clash at the beginning of the *Gavotta*, where the horn C♯ is heard against the D in the oboe [x – **the candidate has forgotten that the horn is a transposing instrument**].
>
> Textures are also quite different from the original by Monza, which was mainly in two parts. Stravinsky scored this movement for woodwinds and brass, seeking to avoid the over-emotional sonorities of the string section [1]. Because he included many more instruments, the textures are obviously thicker, and they become even more thick when Stravinsky adds

There is much good detail here, but alas it is all irrelevant. 'Traditional' harmony is not precise enough at this level to gain credit, and strictly speaking modulation and changes of key come under the heading of tonality.

One of the striking aspects about the harmony of the Gavotta is that all the cadences are perfect.

Try to avoid 'thick' and 'thin' as descriptions of textures at this level.

extra lines, especially obvious in Variation 1 at bar 50 where
the second oboe is given a new part [1 – **illustrated point**].
 In many ways, Stravinsky retains original aspects
of the Monza with trills and the like, though he does
sometimes make the melody jerkier than it was in the 18th-
century version.

Examiner's points

The candidate made four partly illustrated points. The answer was well-written, but marred by irrelevance. Harmony should primarily concern chord structure, chord progressions (including cadences) and dissonance treatment. The answer would gain a mark of **5/13**.

Exercise

Help the candidate raise their mark by suggesting a further two harmonic and two textural points, with appropriate illustrations.

Sample answer 2

Mark this answer yourself, commenting at the end on its good points, but also mentioning ways in which it could have been improved. After completing your marking, check your assessment against the examiner's points below.

 Stravinsky's score is the first of his neoclassical works, and the start
of what proved to be the longest creative phase of his career, lasting over
30 years and culminating with *The Rake's Progress* in 1951.
 There were already hints of this style in the preceding years, e.g.
The Soldier's Tale, so it could be said that Diaghilev should have realised
what he was in for.
 The basis for *Pulcinella* was a series of pieces by Gallo, Pergolesi and
Monza, among others, but instead of simply arranging them, Stravinsky
're-composed' them, as he put it.
 Gavotta and two variations was based on a keyboard work by Monza,
and its basic two-part texture was expanded for the woodwind and brass
sections of the band. Stravinsky had already used this sort of group in his
Symphonies for Wind Instruments, and many other works of the 1920s make
more use of these parts of the orchestra at the expense of the strings, e.g. the
Piano Concerto and *Symphony of Psalms*, as part of an anti-Romantic reaction.
 The expansion of the original to involve several instruments meant
additional melody lines and doublings. Some of these additions include the
Alberti bass in Variation 2, the rapid runs in the flute and the additional
melody lines, e.g. the horn figures in the main theme at bar 11 and the
additional oboe lines at bar 51.
 Stravinsky also introduced some unusual timbres, notably the glissando
effects in the bassoon and the rather high horn parts.

Many of the textural additions have some bearing on the harmony. Inevitably, this is basically traditional with cadential progressions, all of which are perfect. But the cadences are frequently undermined, e.g. right at the end which fizzles out with an open octave, while in the first-time bar, the dominant chord is not followed by a full tonic chord, but a thinly textured return to the Alberti figuration.

Other ways that Stravinsky peps up the harmony involve the adding of pedals, e.g. at bars 26–28, where the inverted tonic pedal sounds right through the perfect cadence, including the dominant chord. Elsewhere he allows a complete clash of D and G chords (bar 44). Additional lines, such as the oboe in bar 51, introduce random unprepared dissonances which sound mildly shocking.

Diaghilev may have been shocked by what Stravinsky did to the 18th-century material, but the result is a great introduction to a particular type of 20th-century style, perfectly matching the mischievous onstage action.

Examiner's points

This well-written account provided good historical context, and incidentally linked the additional textural elements to the harmonic style. The credit-worthy points were:

➢ Woodwind and brass instrumentation

➢ Anti-Romantic reaction

➢ Alberti bass (location given)

➢ Rapid flute runs (not located)

➢ Additional melody lines (illustrated point)

➢ Bassoon glissandi (not located)

➢ High horn parts (not located)

➢ Perfect cadences (not located)

➢ Undermining of cadences (illustrated point)

➢ Pedals (illustrated point)

➢ Superimposed D and G chords (location given)

➢ Unprepared dissonance (location given).

There were 12 points, some of which were illustrated. The essay would gain full marks.

Exercise

Collect information on the harmony and texture in the Sinfonia and Vivo.

SAMPLE QUESTION 2

Describe those aspects of *Morse on the Case* that make it suitable as a piece of incidental music for a television drama. (13)

Before studying the mark scheme (indicative content) that follows, attempt the question yourself.

Indicative content	
Function	The music is designed to be both atmospheric and unobtrusive.
Dynamics	Generally soft throughout.
Resources	Limited to strings, harp, piano, oboe and four horns.
Rhythm	Little movement; lengthy, sustained notes; little sense of pulse; silent bar.
Melody	• Limited amount of melodic material • Mainly diatonic, with few chromatic notes • Gradual unfolding of lines built of perfect 4ths, minor 3rds, major 2nds • Although difficult to hear, there is use of e.g. inversion and diminution (reflecting the thoughtful side of the main character).
Harmony and tonality	• There is no sense of functional progression or a strong drive to cadence • 'Harmony' consists mainly of verticalisations of the component intervals (i.e. chords composed of the notes of the basic motifs) • It is therefore mildly dissonant for the most part • The chromatic notes, especially A♭, produce more stringent clashes, with e.g. A♭ in oboe and A♮ in viola at bars 93–95 (perhaps indicating an intensification in the dramatic situation) • The excerpt eventually moves from A Aeolian to a C major chord at bar 110 (perhaps hinting at a possible resolution in the drama) • But the F♯s, e.g. bars 105 and 108, perhaps suggest the Lydian mode (indicating a brightening of the prevailing mood) • The final chord is ambiguous as it lacks the 3rd.
Structure	There is no discernible structure; the excerpt appears to be through-composed to reflect the on-screen events.
Texture	Pheloung avoids tutti passages, with a sparing use of resources being evident throughout: • Upper strings play throughout, but cellos and bass appear only at bar 99 • Piano plays intermittently throughout, playing variously single notes, two notes, parallel 9ths (bar 36), and five notes on one occasion (bar 98) • The four horns are only used together from bar 98.

Sample answer 1

The music is unobtrusive so it does not overwhelm the screen action [1].
This subtle approach is evident in:
1.   The limited number of instruments [1]
2.   The generally soft dynamics [1]
3.   The lack of a strong, distracting pulse [1]
4.   The very limited amount of melodic material [1]
5.   The vague harmonisations and tonal scheme [x – **not enough**],
      and the chord without a 3rd at the end [1 – **illustrated point**].

Examiner's points

The candidate sets up the makings of a sound answer with the opening assertion and series of follow-up points. Unfortunately, there is an absence of substantiating information and examples, and so the mark is not as high as it could have been. The candidate made six points with limited illustration, and so the final mark would be **6/13**.

> ### Exercise
>
> Suggest some ways in which the main points could have been elaborated.

Sample answer 2

Mark this answer yourself, commenting at the end on its good points, but also mentioning ways in which it could have been improved. After completing your marking, check your assessment against the examiner's points below.

Pheloung provided music for all the Morse dramas, and established a distinctive and effective approach to the writing of incidental music for detective programmes. Pheloung's music is almost self-effacing. Apart from the well-known signature tune, based on Morse code, there is nothing which attracts immediate attention. The music fades in and out as required, and the dynamic level is always soft. The rhythmic scheme is hardly discernible. Notes are long, often being tied across several bars, and it is virtually impossible to detect first beats of the bar or any other strong stresses.

It is also difficult to detect melodic shapes. It is only when you look at the score that you can appreciate the way Pheloung developed the limited number of motifs he employs. At the start there is a simultaneous inversion of the opening motif made up of intervals of a rising 4th and falling minor 3rd, while later he diminishes the cell made up of 2nds and 4ths (see bar 26).

Just as the rhythms and motifs are rather indeterminate, the approach to harmony and tonality is vague. There is in fact little clear harmony, the lines simply coming together at times. Dissonances are far from harsh, with only the Ab on oboe really clashing as it is a chromatic note within the prevailing Aeolian mode. At the end there is perhaps more clarity as the music shifts from A to C, but it is difficult to detect much of a tonal centre. The F♯ perhaps makes it seem like the Lydian mode for a moment, but the final chord which lacks a 3rd makes it impossible to detect a prevailing mode.

Because of the unobtrusive nature of the writing, Pheloung's score is ideal as incidental music, especially for stories that focus on the musings of the central character.

Examiner's points

This was a good, sound attempt, and credit could be awarded for the following points:

➢ 'Self-effacing… nothing which attracts immediate attention'

➢ Soft dynamic level throughout (location given)

➢ Hardly discernible rhythms with long notes and their effects on the stress scheme (not located)

➢ Difficulty in detecting melodic shapes and the limited number of motifs

➢ Simultaneous inversion at the start (location given)

➢ Diminution (illustrated point)

➢ Random harmonic movement

➢ Chromatic Ab (not located)

➢ Aeolian mode

➢ C Lydian at the end (location given)

➢ Final chord without a 3rd (location given).

The essay would be awarded a mark of **11–12/13**. The writing was good, and there was evidence of careful planning and organisation.

Exercise

The candidate did not mention structure or use of resources. Insert a further paragraph to cover these aspects of the music.

INSTRUMENTAL MUSIC 2012 (SECTION C)

SAMPLE QUESTION 1

Compare and contrast the use of rhythm and harmony in the works listed below. (36)

➢   Berlioz – *Harold in Italy*: movement III

➢   Cage – *Sonatas and Interludes for Prepared Piano*: Sonatas I–III

➢   Ram Narayan (India) – *Rag Bhairav*

Before studying the mark scheme (indicative content) that follows, attempt the question yourself. Notice that the key words are *rhythm* and *harmony*. You may find it convenient to refer briefly to the context of each work, but take care to keep your remarks relevant. Points should be illustrated with examples (i.e. bar references) from the music. At a basic level you could just list relevant features of each work, but you may like to try to go further by drawing attention to common features (e.g. stating whether all of the works use drones).

Indicative content	
Rhythm	**Berlioz**
	• Opens with $\frac{6}{8}$ saltarello dance rhythms, with frequent dotted rhythms and stresses on the second beat of the bar
	• The second section is in a slower $\frac{6}{8}$ with some bars appearing to be in $\frac{3}{4}$
	• The idée fixe is in longer notes, chiefly dotted minims
	• All rhythmic elements are heard together at bar 166
	• Augmentation in bars 192–193.
	Cage
	• Inaudible fractal/micro-macrocosmic scheme in which small-scale rhythmic durations determine the overall proportions of the structure
	• Sonata I uses seven-crotchet units in sets of 4 1 3 (repeated); 4 2 (repeated)
	• Sonata II: 1½ + 1½ + 2⅜ + 2⅜ applied to 31 crotchets
	• Sonata III: 1 + 1 + 3¼ + 3¼ applied to 34 crotchets
	• At surface level, the sonatas are marked by: off-beat effects; triplets; other irregular note groupings; rhythmic displacements of short patterns; frequent changes of time signature.
	Rag Bhairav
	• The piece moves from slow, rhythmically free improvisation to music with a clear pulse and energetic rhythmic patterns:
	• Lines 1–13: rhythmically free section (alap)
	• Lines 14–18: jhor with more discernible pulse

	• Lines 19–end: jhala with tabla
	• The tal here is based on a tintal (16-beat rhythmic cycle), subdivided into four vibhag of four beats each
	• Increasingly florid elaborations involve: various types of dotted rhythm; triplets; shorter note values; 'irregular' groupings.
Harmony	**Berlioz** Functional, with cadences; double pedal (drone) in saltarello; secondary 7ths; diminished 7ths; chromaticism. **Cage** Traditional harmonic procedures are impossible because of the effects of preparation. There are no cadences, and only occasional discernible chord structures: • The opening 7th chord of Sonata I • The parallel chords in Sonata I (bar 20). **Rag Bhairav** There is properly speaking no harmony as such, only the drone provided by the tampura.

Sample answer 1

This selection of works makes for an interesting set of comparisons, though whether anything useful will emerge is a completely different matter. Naturally the methods of these composers are bound to be radically opposed to each other as they come from different periods and backgrounds: Berlioz as a 19th-century Romantic, Cage as one of the most anti-traditional composers of the 20th century, and the Rag as an example of Northern Indian chamber music.

> A fair opening paragraph, quickly establishing some context.

Rhythm in the Berlioz is initially governed by the choice of the saltarello dance as the basis of the outer sections of the movement [1]. In $\frac{6}{8}$, it is typified by lively dotted rhythms [1] and occasional off-beat stresses [1]. The central portion of the movement – the serenade proper – moves at a more sedate pace and involves running semiquavers in some of the accompaniment part as well as the solo viola line [1]. The viola also introduces the idée fixe in much longer notes [1]. One of the most striking parts of the movement comes when Berlioz superimposes the saltarello melody and rhythms with the serenade and the idée fixe [1].

> These are valid points, but remember to give bar numbers wherever possible for substantiating examples!

In the Berlioz symphony, rhythm is only one of many elements, but in Cage's Sonatas it is almost the dominant feature. Time signatures are constantly changing [1], and Cage also applies a fractal system, a micro-macrocosmic approach which means that rhythmic proportions also control the structure [1]. In the case of Sonata I, this is seven crotchet units in sets of 4:1:3 (repeated) and 4:2 (repeated) which leads to an opening section of 28 beats (bars 1–7), followed by one bar of only seven crotchets, and then bars 9–12 amounting to 21 beats [1 – **illustrated point**].

> A good connecting idea.

Rhythm is put to different use in *Rag Bhairav*. The first part (lines 1–13) is a rhythmically free improvisation where the main melodic ideas are announced [1]. As the piece progresses, the rhythmic drive intensifies, first in the Jhor [1], and finally in the Jhala, where the tabla is introduced [1 – **location given**]. The tabla provides a tal, or rhythmic cycle of 16 beats, consisting of four sets of four [1]. Rhythms here become increasingly lively, with sometimes irregular groupings [1].

> The location here – 'in the Jhor' – is not sufficiently precise.

> Reference to the entry of the tabla indirectly gives the location.

Harmony in the Berlioz is initially affected by the use of the saltarello in order to show the folk origins of the dance. This is clear from the drone on C and G which runs through the first 31 bars [1 – **illustrated point**], over which Berlioz uses a limited range of chords. In the Serenade, more conventional harmonies occur, but Berlioz does not always follow the expected progressions [1]. In the final stages, effective use is made of a much more relaxed harmonic rhythm, and in fact the harmonic element seems to be faded out of the music before the end [1 – **accept**].

> Examples would be good here.

In the case of Cage, it is much more difficult to discuss harmony. The preparations to the piano often so distort the sounds that the written chords sound completely different from what was expected [1]. Harmony is most evident in Sonata I. It opens with what look like 7th chords on G [1 – **illustrated point**], and at the end there is a stream of parallel chords [1 – **illustrated point**], which here do sound more or less as might be expected. Elsewhere, there is scarcely anything truly harmonic.

In *Rag Bhairav*, the only harmonic device is the drone which supports the melodic material throughout [1 – **location given**].

Examiner's points

This was a sound attempt, standing on the borderline between 'confident' and 'excellent'. 21 points were made, but not all of them were fully illustrated. In terms of organisation, it would have been a good idea to try to draw the threads together in a concluding paragraph, so ensuring a higher mark within the relevant band. In other respects, it was well-constructed. It would receive a mark in the region of **27/36**.

Exercise

Provide a concluding paragraph. You could try to draw threads together by commenting on the Indian influence on Cage, and the extent to which they are reflected in the Sonatas. Are there any common features linking *Harold in Italy* with *Rag Bhairav*?

Sample answer 2

Mark this answer yourself, commenting at the end on its good points, but also mentioning ways in which it could have been improved. After completing your marking, check your assessment against the examiner's points below.

It is surprising to observe the number of links between these widely differing works. *Rag Bhairav* and *Harold in Italy*: movement III immediately seem to have one thing in common: a drone that accompanies their melodic material. In the case of *Rag Bhairav*, it is present throughout, and so there is effectively no harmonic progression as such, so leaving the music to develop entirely through melodic and rhythmic elements. In the case of the Cage, there also seems to be something like a drone at the start of Sonata III, but because of the preparation of the piano you can never be sure of what you are hearing. It does not go on for very long either, and generally there is not much in the way of proper harmony in Cage's pieces. There is two-part writing in Sonata II and three strands towards the end, but it is only in Sonata I that he writes proper chords, such as the G^7 at the start and the series of parallel chords.

The rhythmic element is important in all three works, but is used in very different ways. It is probably most exciting in *Rag Bhairav*, as the players move from free ad-libbing in the first section to increasingly wild and fast rhythms at the end, evident as the tabla comes in. The tabla part is nothing like as complicated as some others, consisting of recurring 16-beat cycles (tintal) of evenly balanced sets of four beats. Against this the sarangi's rhythms become increasingly complex, with many irregular groups of fast-moving notes.

Rhythms in the Berlioz are straightforward with the saltarello dance so prominent. This is a lively dance from the south of Italy, and here Berlioz uses the typical dotted-rhythm figures. The *Serenade* is much calmer, and gives us a peaceful interlude in a contrasting style. The Cage is the most complex of the three as its time signature is constantly changing, and there are all sorts of contrasting groups, e.g. triplets, quintuplets, septuplets, etc.

Examiner's points

The credit-worthy points were as follows:

➢ Drones in both *Harold in Italy* and *Rag Bhairav* (credit for both, with illustrated point for *Rag Bhairav*)

➢ Accept the point about the drones in Sonata III (location given)

➢ Chord G⁷ at the start of Sonata I (illustrated point)

➢ Parallel chords in Sonata I (illustrated point, but not located)

➢ Free ad-libbing in the first section of *Rag Bhairav* (not precisely located)

➢ More rhythmic activity at the entry of the tabla (location given)

➢ 16-beat tintal

➢ Irregular groups of fast-moving notes (illustrated point)

➢ Saltarello dance rhythms in *Harold in Italy* (not located)

➢ Changing time signatures in the Sonatas (not located)

➢ Triplets, quintuplets and septuplets in the Sonatas (not located).

The essay was not very well-organised, and not all of the 12 points made were properly illustrated or located. It seemed that the candidate was attempting some interesting comparisons at the outset, but the attempt was largely unsuccessful because of the lack of system and detailed information. The work falls into the 'adequate' category and would receive **19/36**.

Exercise

Re-organise the essay above so that the information is presented in a much more systematic manner. Find examples to substantiate the un-illustrated points.

SAMPLE QUESTION 2

Compare and contrast the use of melody and texture in the works listed below (36).

➢ **Sweelinck – *Pavana Lachrimae***

➢ **Corelli – Trio Sonata in D, Op. 3 No. 2: movement IV**

➢ **Shostakovich – String Quartet No. 8, Op. 110: movement I**

Before studying the mark scheme (indicative content) that follows, attempt the question yourself. Notice that the key words are *melody* and *texture*. You may find it convenient to refer briefly to the context of each work, but take care to keep your remarks relevant. Points should be illustrated with examples (i.e. bar references) from the music.

Indicative content	
Melody	**Sweelinck**
	• Transfer of vocal styles to keyboard
	• Extensive conjunct movement
	• Descending ('falling tears') line spanning a perfect 4th, sometimes a diminished 4th
	• Rapid semiquaver ornamentation of melodic material
	• Notated trills
	• Minor key with modal elements and variable scales
	• Occasional use of sequence.
	Corelli
	Major key; mainly 3rds and stepwise movement; fragmentation; inversion; sequence.
	Shostakovich
	In a low tessitura throughout; often chromatic; DSCH motif; quotations from earlier works (e.g. Symphony No. 1); appoggiaturas; conjunct movement; narrow-range motives; repetition; sequence.
Texture	**Sweelinck**
	Idiomatic keyboard style, involving a range of textures: free counterpoint; imitation of melody in inner parts; antiphony/dialogue between 6ths in right hand and 3rds in left hand; three-part imitation.
	Corelli
	Polarised; fugal elements; some homorhythm; stretto.
	Shostakovich
	• Low tessituras throughout
	• Four-part imitation
	• DSCH in octaves with internal pedal on viola
	• Two-part counterpoint
	• Homophony
	• Drone and melody in violin I
	• Pedal supporting accompanying figures and melody
	• Chord in upper parts with melody in cello
	• Four-part free counterpoint.

Sample answer 1

The basic melody in Sweelinck's *Pavana Lachrimae* is actually by Dowland, being originally a pavane to which he fitted the words of *Flow My Tears*. Appropriately, it is in minor mode with modal inflections [1], and is typified by falling stepwise lines [1], representing the falling lines of the verse. There are occasional expressive leaps, e.g. the rising minor 6th in bar 2 [1 – **illustrated point**]. Sweelinck's contribution was to provide a variation for each strain involving rapid semiquaver runs [1].

In contrast Corelli's melodic lines are in a major key [1], and generally consist of a combination of stepwise movement and relatively small leaps – most usually 3rds [1]. Corelli extends the line with sequences [1] and also uses inversion in bar 20 [1 – **location given**].

In his String Quartet, Shostakovich uses a cipher based on his own initials [1] – D is short for Dmitry, and he arrives at E♭ as in German musical notation it is called Es, which gives him the S. C is C and B♮ is H. This gives SCH at the end of the German form of his name. Another famous cipher is B♭–A–C–B♮ which spells Bach. Shostakovich also draws on some of his other works, for example, Symphony No. 1 at bar 19 [1 – **illustrated point**] and a descending line taken from Symphony No. 5 [1 – **illustrated point**]. The reason for this self-quotation was perhaps because the quartet almost became a suicide note as Shostakovich was depressed at having been forced to join the Russian communist party. Given the gloomy nature of the background to the work, it is not surprising that the melodies are often in a minor key [1] and use expressive features such as appoggiaturas [1].

Textures in Sweelinck's work vary throughout. The *Pavana* opens with a sort of melody and accompaniment with the accompaniment in a form of free counterpoint [1]. In the middle section there is dialogue between the hands [1] and imitation [1].

Corelli's Trio Sonata has a typical Baroque polarised texture, with two high violin parts and a much lower bass part [1]. As is usual, the bass is doubled by a continuo instrument, in this case an organ, which supplies supporting harmonies [1]. Again, there is a variety of textures, ranging from imitation [1], homorhythm [1] and stretto [1].

The extensive commentary on ciphers and the autobiographical origins of the work are out of proportion in an essay of this scope. Always try to keep remarks relevant.

Apart from giving bar references, there is more to be said about the dialogue, e.g. the intervals used in the right hand as opposed to the left. In the case of the imitation, how many voices are involved?

Shostakovich's quartet is also highly varied. It opens imitatively with a series of entries built on DSCH [1 – **location given**]. There are passages involving two-part counterpoint [1], and also a lengthy section of melody with drone [1]. The very low instrumental ranges also contribute to the gloom which is typical of this movement [1].

Examiner's points

Apart from a couple of excessively longwinded digressions, much of this essay was clearly focused on the demands of the question. The candidate made 25 relevant observations, but unfortunately not all of these were adequately substantiated. In view of this, the essay would be considered 'confident', and be awarded a mark in the region of **25/36**.

Exercise

Provide an introduction and conclusion to the essay.

Sample answer 2

Mark this answer yourself, commenting at the end on its good points, but also mentioning ways in which it could have been improved. After completing your marking, check your assessment against the examiner's points below.

Though nearly four centuries separate the composition of the earliest and latest works in this question, there are remarkable similarities in approaches to both melody and texture.

Sweelinck was well-acquainted with the work of a number of English composers who worked on the continent, and there is good reason to believe he adopted some of the keyboard techniques of such composers as John Bull in his own writing. Not only that, he used as the basis for *Pavana Lachrimae* the lute-song 'Flow my tears' by the English composer John Dowland, who also spent some time abroad, mainly at the Danish court.

The melancholy atmosphere of *Pavana Lachrimae*, like that of the original it was based on, lies partly in the use of the minor key and the measured pace associated with the pavane. The melodic lines fall by step, so symbolising the falling tears of Dowland's text. In addition there are sequential repeats, for example bars 2–4 are a higher version of the line in bars 1–2. There is also in bar 2 an expressive leap of a minor 6th.

In effect, Sweelinck was limited by Dowland's material, but he repeated each strain with variations that feature running semiquavers and ornamentations, such as the written-out trill in bar 14.

The textures in *Pavana Lachrimae* go beyond a simple melody-and-accompaniment. At the start the lower parts are freely contrapuntal, and later on there is antiphonal exchange between the hands at bar 40, where the 6ths in the right hand answer the 3rds in the left. There is also imitation for three of the four parts at bar 43 onwards.

Melody in Sweelinck's piece is obviously vocal in origin, whereas in Corelli it is much more idiomatic. It covers a wide range, though at any one time it tends to involve conjunct movement or intervals of a 3rd. Corelli breaks up the main theme, for example the quaver motif picked out at bar 11, and also uses inversion (bar 20) and sequence (bars 8–10). The textures seem at first to be fugal, as violin II comes in with a sort of answer, and there is also use of stretto at bar 21 where the subject comes in after only one bar.

The melody in the Shostakovich is sometimes based on the DSCH cipher – D, E♭, C, B – which stands for an abbreviation of the composer's name. It appears at the start in a series of imitative entries, starting with the lowest of the four instruments. It also appears in a purely homophonic texture (bar 79). Shostakovich also uses a melody and drone. His melodies are often chromatic, and so differ greatly from Corelli's.

Examiner's points

The candidate here provided a large amount of relevant information, with credit being earned for:

Sweelinck:

➤ Falling conjunct lines

➤ Sequence (illustrated)

➤ Minor 6th (located)

➤ Running semiquavers

➤ Ornamentation (illustrated)

➤ Freely contrapuntal at the start (located)

➤ Antiphony at bar 40 (located)

➤ Imitation at bar 43 (located).

Corelli:

➤ Conjunct writing, with 3rds

➤ Breaking up of main theme (illustrated)

➤ Inversion (located)

➤ Sequence (located)

➤ Fugal textures

➤ Stretto (located).

Shostakovich:

➤ DSCH

➤ Imitative entries (located)

➤ Homophony (located)

➤ Melody and drone

➤ Chromaticism.

Many of these points were substantiated by way of bar references. Unfortunately, the candidate perhaps spent so much time establishing the background to Sweelinck's approach that they seemed to run out of time. A number of additional points could have been made in the final paragraphs, and the essay would have benefited from some concluding remarks. It would however fall into the 'excellent' category, and earn a mark in the region of **27/36**.

Exercise

Shorten the second paragraph, provide some further information on Shostakovich and write a concluding paragraph.

APPLIED MUSIC 2013 (SECTION B)

SAMPLE QUESTION 1

Describe features of Gabrieli's *Sonata pian' e forte* that are typical of Venetian Renaissance music. (13)

Before studying the mark scheme (indicative content) that follows, attempt the question yourself. Notice that the 'key words' are *Venetian* and *Renaissance*, so you should think about the circumstances of performance as well as the more general Renaissance features of the work. The question is open-ended; in other words, it does not specify particular features to be described. In such cases, try to comment on rhythm, melody, harmony, tonality, texture, performing forces and genre or structure. Points should be illustrated with examples from the music.

> Because you take an unmarked copy of the anthology into the exam room, your examples should normally be bar and part references where appropriate. You will gain no further credit for copying out passages of music, and will merely lose valuable time.

Indicative content	
Rhythm	• Limited variety of note lengths
	• Final part of the piece uses shorter note lengths
	• Syncopation.
Melody	• Relatively restricted range
	• Frequently conjunct, the largest interval being an octave, with 4ths and 5ths occurring more frequently.
Harmony	• Root-position and first-inversion chords dominate, with an occasional consonant 4th
	• Cadences include perfect, imperfect (Phrygian) and plagal
	• Tierces de Picardie
	• Various suspensions.

Tonality	Dorian mode on G. Cadences on various degrees of the mode producing a 'wandering' tonality.
Texture	Polychoral; antiphonal; mainly contrapuntal, with some occasional homophony; imitation.
Resources	• Uses typical Renaissance instruments – cornett, old violin (with a range similar to the modern viola) and trombones (or sackbuts) • Writing is not yet idiomatic, the music showing signs of 'vocal' styles.
Structure	Through-composed, so revealing links with sacred vocal works (e.g. motet).
Context	Designed for performance in St Mark's Basilica, Venice, thus allowing use of spatially separated galleries, in this case involving two four-part groups.

As previously mentioned, examiners arrive at a final mark for these questions using a holistic grid. For full details see Edexcel's *Sample Assessment Materials*. For the present, it is enough to know that the full 13 marks will be awarded to work which contains at least nine relevant, well-illustrated points, showing excellent organisation and planning, and expressed coherently without significant spelling or grammatical errors.

As you work through this section of the book, and see examples of work of different standards, you will see how the holistic grid is applied across the available mark range.

Sample answer 1

Gabrieli's work stands on the borderlines of Renaissance and Baroque music. Some works, such as the motet *In ecclesiis*, show definite signs of the Baroque with the use of continuo instruments and the combination of voices and instruments. In contrast, *Sonata pian' e forte* is quite old-fashioned and in many ways shows stylistic traits of the Renaissance era. ◄———

> A good opening paragraph, establishing the historical context.

This is immediately apparent in the instrumental writing. Although Gabrieli specified particular instruments, such as violin, cornett and trombones, his writing for them is not idiomatic, and in fact looks more as though it derives from vocal models [1], especially the sacred music of the 16th century. This in itself has an influence on the nature of the melodic writing. Stepwise writing is frequent [1], and leaps are rarely more than a 4th or 5th [1].

Harmony and tonality also contain aspects that point towards the Renaissance. The work is modal, being written in the Dorian mode on G [1]. Gabrieli cadences on most steps of the Dorian scale, leading to a fluid tonal scheme, for example G at bar 25, C at bar 31, B♭ at bar 43 and D at bar 54 [1 – **illustrated point**]. Cadences include perfect (e.g. bar 25), Phrygian (bars 16–17) and plagal at the end [3 – **locations given**]. As often happens in music of this period, a tierce de Picardie is frequently used at the end of sections, and also at the end of the work [1 – **location given**].

Texture is also typically Renaissance. Often the music is contrapuntal [1], and from bar 71, there is a series of close imitations [1 – **location given**] in most of the eight parts, contributing to much of the excitement in the closing stages of the work.

The characteristically Venetian aspects of the music come with the division of the eight parts into two groups of four instruments. These would have been placed in separate galleries in St Mark's, Venice [1], where Gabrieli was organist and director of music. It allows him scope for striking antiphonal exchanges [1] and grandiose tuttis.

Overall, the work is highly typical both of Venetian methods of the times and older Renaissance music in general.

Examiner's points

This was a very good answer with 13 observations, many of which were well-substantiated. It was coherent and well-expressed, and would have been awarded full marks. Notice that not all observations can usefully be supported by examples, for example the general point that the work is in the Dorian mode in G. There is indeed little point in giving examples of features which occur throughout, such as stepwise movement.

Exercise

List further features that the candidate could have included.

Sample answer 2

Mark this answer yourself, commenting at the end on its good points, but also mentioning ways in which it could have been improved. After completing your marking, check your assessment against the examiner's points below.

> *Sonata pian' e forte* shows many features of Renaissance music. It is modal as it is in the Dorian mode, transposed to G, and the harmony is characterised by almost constant use of Picardy thirds, e.g. at the end.
>
> Textures are clearly Renaissance in style, being mainly contrapuntal. Much of this counterpoint is free, with the parts independent of each other, but Gabrieli also uses some imitation, particularly near the end.
>
> Rhythms are typical of this period as they are rather simple, though again at bar 71 things become more complicated, and there is even some syncopation (in the cornett).
>
> An important feature of *Sonata pian' e forte* is the use of antiphony. This often occurs in Venetian music as the building the music was meant to be played in – St Mark's – has widely-spaced galleries for musicians. This was ideal for playing off different groups against each other.

Examiner's points

The credit-worthy points are as follows:

➤   Modal, Dorian in G

➤   Tierce de Picardie (location given)

➤   Contrapuntal

➤   Imitation (but the location was insufficiently precise for credit)

➤   Basic rhythms

➤   Syncopation at bar 71 (location given)

➤   Antiphony

➤   St Mark's galleries.

The total was eight points, not all illustrated when possible. Such a response is regarded as competent. The writing was coherent, though it would have been possible to deal with textural features (counterpoint and antiphony) together. Clearly, very much more could have been included. The final mark would be **8/13**.

> ## Exercise
>
> List additional points that the candidate could have made. Provide a final 'summarising' sentence to round off the answer.

SAMPLE QUESTION 2

Identify rhythmic and melodic features of *Baris Melampahan* that indicate that it is an example of gamelan music. (13)

Before studying the mark scheme (indicative content) that follows, attempt the question yourself. Notice that the key words are *rhythm*, *melody* and *gamelan*. You may find it convenient to refer briefly to the work's context, but take care to keep your remarks relevant. Do not waste time on any aspect of *Baris Melampahan* that is not to do with rhythm and melody.

Indicative content	
Rhythm	• Regular pulse throughout • Until the slowing down at the end of the extract • Constant on-beat pulse • With some off-beat sounds from the reyong and kendhang • Rhythms are occasionally displaced • Organised in rhythmic cycles – gongans • Consisting of four ketegs • Each keteg lasts four beats • Gongs mark the end of each cycle.
Melody	• Based on a 'nuclear' melody • Involving pitch numbers 1, 2, 3, 5 and 6 from the pelog scale • This pentatonic version of the scale is known as the pelog selisir • Difficult to describe component intervals because of the tuning that differs from e.g. European tuning • Frequent repetitions • Heard in varying degrees of completion • The only significant departure occurs at [H], the 'high tune'.

Sample answer 1

Rhythm
➢ Gongs mark divisions between the cycles [1]
➢ The cycles are called gongans [1]
➢ They consist of four ketegs [1]
➢ Ombak effects.

Melody
➤   Nuclear melody [1]
➤   Treated heterophonically
➤   Alternates with angsel and kendhang [1]
➤   Based on five pitches – selisir pelog [1].

Examiner's points

The candidate made six basic points in a rather sketchy way. At most, the answer would gain **7/13**.

> **Exercise**
>
> Rewrite the candidate's statements in continuous prose to remove ambiguity.

Sample answer 2

Mark this answer yourself, commenting at the end on its good points, but also mentioning ways in which it could have been improved. After completing your marking, check your assessment against the examiner's points below.

The war-like qualities of this piece, played by a group based right in the central region of Bali, are conveyed by the insistent rhythms, maintained until the very end of the extract where there is a slowing down. The music has a distinct four-beat feel, and each rhythmic cycle (gongan) consists of four four-beat bars or ketegs.

The overall impression is quite different from western music as the instruments are tuned differently. In fact tuning varies from region to region, and the impression is further complicated by the fact that the metallophones are often slightly out of tune with each other, producing the ombak effect.

Gamelan music is based on the pelog scale. This consists of seven notes, but in this case the music draws on only five pitches (C♯, D, E, G♯, A) as given in the preface in the anthology, though these pitches are only very approximate. At some points, the music moves into a higher pitch region ('the high tune'), but the group sticks to the same basic pitches, an octave higher.

The tune is initially heard on the ugal, the largest of the two-octave metallophones, and later is heard decorated on the gangsa, sangsih and polos, producing the heterophonic effect which is so characteristic of gamelan music. The basic four-bar phrase is often repeated, producing the characteristic hypnotic effect of this music.

This is communal music, and the whole village takes part in the performance.

Examiner's points

Credit would be awarded for mention of:

➢ Insistent rhythms

➢ Slowing down at end of the piece (location given)

➢ Gongans

➢ Ketegs

➢ Four four-beat cycles

➢ Tuning

➢ Five-note scale

➢ Higher pitches

➢ Repetition.

There are nine points with little illustration. It was well-written, but marred by some irrelevance. It would gain **10/13**.

> **Exercise**
>
> Draw up revision notes for this piece on texture, timbre, structure and circumstances of performance.

INSTRUMENTAL MUSIC 2013 (SECTION C)

SAMPLE QUESTION 1

Compare and contrast the use of harmony and tonality in the three pieces listed below. (36)

➢ **Haydn – String Quartet in E♭, Op. 33 No. 2, 'The Joke': movement IV**

➢ **Brahms – Piano Quintet in F minor, Op. 34: movement III**

➢ **Miles Davis Quintet –** *Four* **(opening).**

Before studying the mark scheme (indicative content) that follows, attempt the question yourself. Notice that the key words are harmony and tonality. You may find it convenient to refer briefly to the context of each work, but take care to keep your remarks relevant. Points should be illustrated with examples from the music.

Indicative content	
Harmony	**Haydn**
	• Functional progressions
	• Cadences (perfect and imperfect)
	• Appoggiatura chords
	• Suspensions
	• Dominant 9th
	• Pedal points (often dominant)
	• Harmonic rhythm varies
	• Unresolved second-inversion chords.
	Brahms
	• Functional progressions
	• Cadences
	• Secondary dominants
	• Pedal points
	• Chromatic chords, e.g. augmented 6ths
	• Occasional open 5th chords.
	Davis
	• Chromaticism
	• 7th chords
	• Parallelism
	• Secondary dominants
	• Circle of 5ths
	• Substitution chords.
Tonality	**Haydn**
	• Limited modulation.
	Brahms
	• Minor, with some modality. A wide-ranging key scheme.
	Davis
	• E♭ throughout, but obscured by many of the harmonic devices listed above.

Sample answer 1

Haydn was Classical, Brahms Romantic and Davis mid-20th century jazz. As about 200 years separate the earliest and latest works, it is only to be expected that there are certain differences between their approaches to harmony and tonality. Partly this is because of developments in forms and instrumentation. Haydn uses a sort of rondo form for the last movement of the quartet, with various episodes and a contrasting slow section near the end. In contrast, Brahms uses a piano with solo strings instead of a Classical orchestra, and the piece itself is a scherzo and trio, a massively expanded version of the minuet and trio, the sort of movement that Haydn would have written. In complete contrast, the Davis piece is a head arrangement specially written to show off his virtuosity as a trumpeter.

> This over-extended introductory paragraph also introduces a number of irrelevant points. The first two sentences would have been sufficient to establish some sort of background.

When we come to a survey of harmony and tonality, the first thing to notice is the fact that Haydn uses functional harmony [1]. This means that the music is in major/minor keys rather than in modes or being atonal, and the chords help to define the keys through the use of cadences. There are four of these: imperfect, perfect, plagal and interrupted, though Haydn uses only the first two listed, e.g. the perfect cadence, consisting of a dominant to tonic progression, as at bars 7–8 [1 – **illustrated point**].

> At last!

> At this level, it will be assumed that you know what the chord progressions making up the cadences are, and there really is no need to specify them.

The imperfect cadence also consists of two chords. The second is the dominant, but we cannot be sure of the first chord until we hear it, as any workable chord is acceptable here. Haydn uses an imperfect cadence at bar 16 [1 – **illustrated point**]. Otherwise his choice of chords is quite limited.

Brahms uses a much wider selection, but there are times when there is hardly any harmony at all. This happens at the start where there is just a simple bass note accompanying the melody lines – a repeated C.

> What is the term for this device?

When the chords come in at bar 22, Brahms changes to C major [1 – **location given**] from F minor [x].

He also uses rhythmic augmentation here to produce a grand effect.

> A frequent misreading of the key at the opening of this movement. The quintet overall is in F minor, but this movement of course opens in C minor.

The harmony here is functional [1] and very rich, as all the instruments are playing. In fact there's a fantastic amount of harmony in the piano part as the pianist has to play lots of notes.

> Irrelevant.

> A nonsensical statement!

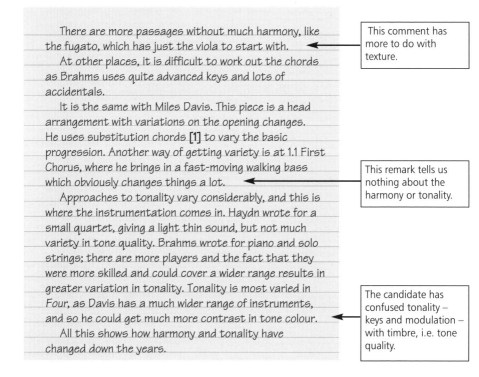

There are more passages without much harmony, like the fugato, which has just the viola to start with. ← This comment has more to do with texture.

At other places, it is difficult to work out the chords as Brahms uses quite advanced keys and lots of accidentals.

It is the same with Miles Davis. This piece is a head arrangement with variations on the opening changes. He uses substitution chords [1] to vary the basic progression. Another way of getting variety is at 1.1 First Chorus, where he brings in a fast-moving walking bass which obviously changes things a lot. ← This remark tells us nothing about the harmony or tonality.

Approaches to tonality vary considerably, and this is where the instrumentation comes in. Haydn wrote for a small quartet, giving a light thin sound, but not much variety in tone quality. Brahms wrote for piano and solo strings: there are more players and the fact that they were more skilled and could cover a wider range results in greater variation in tonality. Tonality is most varied in Four, as Davis has a much wider range of instruments, and so he could get much more contrast in tone colour. ← The candidate has confused tonality – keys and modulation – with timbre, i.e. tone quality.

All this shows how harmony and tonality have changed down the years.

Examiner's points

The candidate made six relevant points. There was extensive irrelevance and confusion, so under these circumstances the final mark would be in the region of 12/36.

> **Exercise**
>
> Write a paragraph contrasting the approaches to tonality in the three works under discussion.

Sample answer 2

Mark this answer yourself, commenting at the end on its good points, but also mentioning ways in which it could have been improved. After completing your marking, check your assessment against the examiner's points below.

Haydn's quartet is in E♭ major. Brahms' Piano Quintet is also in a minor key (C). Four is in a major key (E♭). All three pieces also have passages in various keys.

Davis uses substitution chords. The harmonies at the start are easy to see: E♭, E♭m⁷, A♭⁷, Fm⁷ and so on.

Haydn doesn't use substitution chords, but he does use diminished 7ths. Brahms modulates to C major at bar 22. Davis does not really use cadences. Haydn doesn't use plagal cadences, but he finishes with a perfect cadence a lot of times, so that we get the message!

Brahms uses remote keys like B major.

Harmony is functional in Brahms. It is in Haydn as well, but is much more chromatic in Four.

Davis uses substitute chords. Like Davis, Haydn finishes in E♭ major. Brahms opens with a tonic pedal – the repeated Cs in the cello. Four is a sort of variation piece built on the opening section.

It is interesting to notice that none of these works has a circle of 5ths, but Brahms does use some augmented 6th chords.

Davis uses pitch bends to vary the harmonies. Haydn also uses a dominant pedal.

Examiner's points

Marks can be awarded here for:

➢ Naming the keys of the Piano Quintet and Four (the key of the string quartet is given in the title, and so would not gain a mark simply for being stated)

➢ Use of substitution chords in Four

➢ Modulation to C at bar 22 in the Piano Quintet (location given)

➢ Perfect cadence at the end of Haydn's movement (location given)

➢ Functional harmony in the Brahms and Haydn

➢ Chromatic harmony in Four

➢ Tonic pedal (location given) and augmented 6th chords in the Brahms

➢ Dominant pedal in the Haydn.

Notice that credit was not awarded for key references which were not located precisely; reading off the chord descriptions from the score of Four; and negative statements.

There was no evidence of planning, the whole piece being little more than a random stringing together of facts, not all of which were fully illustrated.

As there were 11 points with limited illustration, but weak organisation, this piece would be awarded **16/36**.

> **Exercise**
>
> Organise the answer above, grouping points together logically and providing bar references where appropriate.

SAMPLE QUESTION 2

Compare and contrast the use of resources and textures in the three pieces listed below. (36)

➢ **Holborne – Pavane 'The image of melancholy' and Galliard 'Ecce quam bonum'**

➢ **Poulenc – Sonata for Horn, Trumpet and Trombone: movement I**

➢ **Reich –** *New York Counterpoint*: **movement II**

Before studying the mark scheme (indicative content) that follows, attempt the question yourself. Notice that the key words are *resources* and *texture*. You may find it convenient to refer briefly to the context of each work, but take care to keep your remarks relevant. Points should be illustrated with examples from the music.

Indicative content	
Resources	Holborne • Playable on any available instrument of the day, i.e. viols, violins or wind instruments – instrumental writing is not idiomatic. Poulenc • Requires modern brass instruments (horn in F, trumpet in C, trombone). Considerable skill required in performance. Reich • Requires live clarinet, with pre-recorded parts for eight clarinets and two bass clarinets (i.e. for a single family of instruments).
Texture	Holborne • Five-part polyphony almost throughout • Equivalent voices (i.e. of equal importance) • Generally contrapuntal • Some imitation • Entries are often concealed (through the absence of rests) • Imitation by inversion • Homophony in central section of the Galliard

- Bass part less active

- Pedals.

Poulenc

- Various forms of melody-dominated homophony

- Occasional bars of monophony

- Melody initially in horn, but sometimes in trumpet

- Broken-chord patterns

- Accompaniment split between trumpet and trombone.

Reich

- Polyphonic

- Imitation, applied to two lines with the same rhythm

- The imitations are close or phased

- Four-part pulsing homophony faded in and out in pairs.

Sample answer 1

A span of three-and-a-half centuries separates the composition of these works, so it is not surprising to find considerable differences in approach to the use of texture. These differences are further magnified by the selection of forces for each work.

Holborne's work is a characteristic example of Renaissance polyphony. Written for five [1] equal parts [1] it is mainly contrapuntal [1]. It involves some imitation [1], but these imitative points are far from easy to hear as Holborne often conceals entries by avoiding preceding rests [1] or else by using inversions (for example bar 1 of the Galliard in the first and fourth lines) [1 – **illustrated point**]. Most of the lines are as lively and melodic as the others, though for harmonic reasons, the bass line is slower moving [1], and even includes pedal-points, for example bars 34–39 of the Pavane [1 – **illustrated point**]. The one significant departure from this basic texture comes with the second section of the Galliard, which is more homophonic [1 – **location given**].

Whereas Holborne's writing was by no means idiomatic [1], and could be performed on any suitable set of instruments, Poulenc's Sonata is intended for the instruments named, and indeed for highly skilled players [1]. Textures are basically melody-dominated

> Notice that the candidate correctly uses the term 'polyphony' here simply to refer to the combination of a number of separate melody lines, and uses 'contrapuntal' in connection with their independence.

> Good point.

homophony [1], but because Poulenc had only three melody instruments available, he uses broken-chord figures (for example at bar 26) to supply harmonic content [1 – **illustrated point**]. The work is often humorous in intent, and this accounts for the splitting of a single-note accompaniment between trombone and trumpet at bar 40 [1 – **illustrated point**]. There are also occasional bars of monophony, for example from bar 21 to bar 25 [1 – **illustrated point**], and a final bar of octaves [1 – **illustrated point**].

Reich's work is markedly different in concept. It is written for a single family of instruments, namely clarinets [1], but he goes further, intending it to be performed by a single player who performs one part to pre-recorded parts for eight clarinets and two bass-clarinets [1]. The result is a rich web of interweaving sound, a sort of polyphony [1]. It is notable for its imitations which are very closely spaced – often only a quaver apart [1]. This technique is known as phasing [1]. Reich fades the textures in and out [1], the only contrast coming part way through when he introduces a series of rapidly repeated semiquaver chords ('pulsing homophony') [1]. These also fade in and out, and gradually change.

These works are typical of their respective eras. There are clear similarities between Holborne's Pavane and Galliard and Reich's New York Counterpoint in that they are both polyphonic, while Poulenc's Sonata is almost entirely homophonic.

Examiner's points

The candidate made 23 often well-illustrated points. The answer had good opening and closing paragraphs, and was efficiently written. The quality of written communication would permit a mark somewhere in the region of **30/36**.

> **Exercise**
>
> Find substantiating examples for those points the candidate did not illustrate.

Sample answer 2

Mark this answer yourself, commenting at the end on its good points, but also mentioning ways in which it could have been improved. After completing your marking, check your assessment against the examiner's points below.

Textures change from one period to another and from one work to another, even within the same period. One of the factors influencing the use of textures is the instruments being used. Holborne's piece is for five instruments and therefore has a thick texture, while the Poulenc is for only three instruments and therefore sounds thin, and Reich's has one instrument but in fact does not sound as thin as expected as it has plenty going on, but not quite as much as Holborne.

So starting with the Holborne, it is quite contrapuntal most of the time. There are five parts, all rather vocal in style, because the music dated from the period before instruments had developed their own techniques. As it says in the anthology, these pieces can be performed on violins, viols or any musical wind instrument (note to examiner: I have translated this into proper English so you won't misunderstand). In other words, these pieces can be played on any instruments, just so long as the notes fit. Most of the parts play a similar role, but it is interesting to see that the bass part has less to do. Probably because it helped the harmony if there was a firm, clear support for what was going on above. The other parts tend to have a very similar style, and because the music is from the Renaissance period, it is contrapuntal. Sometimes Holborne also uses imitations, and sometimes he uses inverted melody lines (see opening of the Galliard). Holborne departs from this approach only in bars 9–16 of the Galliard which is more chordal. This movement is in the minor key and closes with a tierce de Picardie as was customary at the time.

The Poulenc Sonata needs really good players. Unlike the Holborne which is not idiomatic, this is now clearly intended for the horn, trumpet and trombone, and they are all so good they take turns in having the tune – well obviously not the trombone as that is a bass instrument. They all come together playing in octaves at the end – which gives a sense of finality.

Finally, New York Counterpoint. This has so much going on that it is a bit of a jumble. The same player plays everything. As it says in the anthology: 'The soloist pre-records eight clarinet and two bass-clarinet parts and then a final 11th part live against the tape'. There is a risk that it can get a bit dull all being on the same type of instrument. All the parts have similar ideas, but they come in at different times in a sort of imitation. There are also parts with repeated semiquavers in the lower instruments which give chords underneath the imitations.

Examiner's points

Credit is awarded for:

Holborne:

Counterpoint; not idiomatic; five parts; slower-moving bass part; imitation; inverted melody lines (location given); middle section of the Galliard more chordal (location given).

Poulenc:

Skilled players; octaves at the end (location given).

Reich:

Same family of instruments; imitation; repeated chords.

The other points were irrelevant. Avoid asides to examiners, however helpful they are meant to be. This work was on the borderline between adequate and competent, with 13 partially illustrated points. It would receive **20/36**.

Exercise

Cut out the irrelevant remarks in the answer above, and add six fully illustrated observations to help raise the mark.

APPLIED MUSIC 2014 (SECTION B)

SAMPLE QUESTION 1

Describe features of 'Quoniam tu solus' from Haydn's Nelson Mass which show that it was intended for an important ceremony in a wealthy cathedral or chapel. (13)

Before studying the mark scheme (indicative content) that follows, attempt the question yourself. Notice that the key words are *important ceremony* and *wealthy cathedral or chapel*, so you should think about how this work differs from more 'ordinary' works of the time. The question is 'open-ended', in other words it does not specify particular features to be described. In this case, try to comment on performing forces and any harmonic, tonal and textural features that suggest a wealthy background and jubilation. Points should be illustrated with examples from the music.

Because you take an unmarked copy of the anthology into the exam room, your examples should normally be bar and part references where appropriate. You will gain no further credit for copying out passages of music, and will merely lose valuable time.

Indicative content	
Background	• One of a series of six masses composed to celebrate the Name Day of the Princess Esterházy • It dates from August 1798, and was first performed that year • 'Quoniam tu solus' is the final section from the Gloria.
Resources	Clearly intended for a large, richly endowed church: • Four solo voices (SATB) • SATB chorus • Orchestra of strings, three clarini trumpets and timpani and organ • Complex music requiring careful rehearsal.
Texture	A wide range of textures is available: • Melody-dominated homophony • Solo soprano in antiphony with the chorus • Independent orchestral parts, with some heterophony. The middle section is a fugato. It includes stretti. The orchestra here doubles the voice parts. The closing section contains: canonic entries in the solo voices; pedal and broken chords in the orchestra; free counterpoint then homophony in the chorus.
Harmony and tonality	• The work is in D major, a key associated with expressions of jubilation (through the use of trumpets) • The jubilant tonality is reinforced with frequent perfect cadences and pedal points • The fugato has a sophisticated tonal scheme, touching on a number of related keys.

Sample answer 1

The fact that this work was performed for the aristocracy in a wealthy chapel is indicated by:

1. Large performing group of four soloists, SATB chorus, orchestra of strings, organ and three trumpets [1 – **illustrated point**].

2. Musically complex textures, requiring some careful rehearsal [1], e.g. string parts ornamenting vocal parts with heterophonic lines – as in bar 6 [1 – **location given**]; fast-moving fugue with three subjects [1] and stretti [1] doubled by orchestra [1]; antiphonal exchange at the start between soprano and choir [1 – **location given**].

3. Ceremonial nature of the music using the key of D major, suitable for trumpets [1].

4. Also the sophisticated tonal scheme of the fugato touching on other keys [1].

5. Jubilant nature of music, stressing D major with pedals [1] and cadences, especially at the end [1].

Examiner's points

This answer covered most of the points that might have been expected, and if the illustrations had been more specific it would have earned full marks. As it is, a mark of **11/13** is appropriate.

Exercise

Supply the missing illustrations, and add a further point briefly explaining the work's original purpose.

Sample answer 2

Mark this answer yourself, commenting at the end on its good points, but also mentioning ways in which it could have been improved. After completing your marking, check your assessment against the examiner's points below.

> The 'Quoniam tu solus sanctus' is the final section of the Gloria, and therefore is one of the most celebratory sections of the Mass. Haydn's setting is even more so, as it could only have been performed by a large group of professional performers. It would have to be mounted in a church with sufficient space and with the necessary resources. This is clear from the relative complexity of the music which would require skilled performers and rehearsal.
>
> The music consists of a series of strongly contrasted sections, all with different textures and with some variety in tonality. The first is broadly homophonic with a four-part choir answering a solo soprano. The orchestral writing, though supportive, is often independent of the vocal parts, with scales and other ornamentations.
>
> The second section has a different approach, as the orchestra doubles the voice parts. It is a fugato which quickly passes through a number of related keys. The other vocal soloists enter in the final part with snatches of canon. It closes in D major, with a number of perfect cadences.
>
> The ceremonial nature of the music arises from the fact that it was written for the Name Day of Princess Esterhazy in 1798.

Examiner's points

The credit-worthy points are as follows:

➢   Last section of the Gloria

➢   Large group of professional performers

➢   Complexity of the music

➢   Wide range of textures

➢ Homophonic choir answering solo soprano (location given)

➢ Independent orchestral writing

➢ Fugato (location given)

➢ Orchestra doubles voices (location given)

➢ Uses a number of related keys

➢ Canon (not precisely located)

➢ Perfect cadences in D major (location given)

➢ Written for Name Day of Princess Esterházy.

12 points are made, although not very well-illustrated, and this work would be deemed 'confident', receiving **10/13**. After a promising start, the answer seemed to lose focus, and obvious details about the resources used were not given.

Exercise

Redraft the answer above so that the question is tackled in a more direct way. Provide substantiating examples where appropriate.

SAMPLE QUESTION 2

Identify characteristic features of steel-band music present in *Yellow Bird*. (13)

Before studying the mark scheme (indicative content) that follows, attempt the question yourself. Notice that the key words are *characteristic* and *steel band*. The question is 'open-ended', in other words it does not specify particular features to be described. In this case, try to comment on performing forces, rhythm, melody, harmony and tonality as well as textural features as appropriate.

Indicative content	
Background	• Based on a calypso piece (a song usually with satirical content)
	• Traditionally performed in Trinidad during Carnival
	• The steel pans are fashioned from oil drums.
Rhythm and metre	• In rapid quadruple time
	• Each part has a different rhythm
	• Syncopations
	• Tango rhythm in the bass.
Melody	• Diatonic
	• Range of a 9th

	• Mainly in four-bar phrases, except for one of five bars
	• Use of sequence
	• Varied repetitions
	• Prominent triadic lines.
Harmony and tonality	• Diatonic: many perfect cadences
	• Primary triads
	• G major with no modulation
	• A small amount of chromaticism.
Structure	• Ax2 – B – Ax2 – B.
Texture	• Steel pans accompanied by drum-kit
	• Rhythmically enlivened melody-dominated homophony
	• Countermelody appears at bar 28
	• Tremolo is used to produce the longer note lengths.

Sample answer 1

The features that make *Yellow Bird* a typical steel-band piece are as follows:
1. It is in calypso style [1] – a typical Trinidadian form
2. The rhythms involve a lot of syncopation [1]. There are also tango rhythms in the bass part [1].
3. The melody has a simple layout, with mainly four-bar phrases [1].
4. The structure is straightforward: ABAB [1 – **accept**].
5. Harmony as well as melody is diatonic [1]. The harmony is made up of primary chords [1].
6. Texture is melody-dominated homophony [1], even though the accompanying parts all have different rhythms [1].

Examiner's points

Nine points are made here, but there is very little illustration. A mark of **9/13** is appropriate.

> **Exercise**
>
> Provide examples where suitable, and expand on points 3 and 5.

Sample answer 2

Mark this answer yourself, commenting at the end on its good points, but also mentioning ways in which it could have been improved. After completing your marking, check your assessment against the examiner's points below.

> The origins of Yellow Bird are immediately clear from the sheer sound of the piece. The sonorities of the steel pans, fashioned from oil drums, point to Trinidad, and also the way longer notes are prolonged through the use of tremolo effects.
>
> Another clue to the origins of the piece is the rhythmic scheme. There are many contrasting patterns in the different parts, but the tango rhythm in the bassline and the frequent syncopations are further proof. The piece is quite clearly a calypso in style, and though we do not have the text it was no doubt humorous or satirical in nature.
>
> The melody is typically diatonic, with triadic patterns and four-bar phrases, much repetition, some sequential, and rather unusually a five-bar phrase as well. The harmony is also relatively simple with primary chords and the occasional 7th. There is only very little passing chromaticism, and the key, which does not change, is constantly reinforced with perfect cadences in G.
>
> Textures seem complex on the surface, with a lot of contrasting rhythms, but the essential scheme is homophonic.

Examiner's points

Credit is available for:

- Steel pans
- Contrasting rhythmic patterns
- Syncopation
- Diatonic melody
- Repetition
- Five-bar phrase
- 7th chords
- Unchanging key
- Homophonic.

- Tremolo
- Tango rhythm
- Calypso style
- Triadic patterns
- Sequence
- Primary chords
- A little chromaticism
- Perfect cadences

Unfortunately, the candidate's work did not quite make it into the highest band because of the failure to offer specific illustrations. A mark of **12/13** is appropriate here.

INSTRUMENTAL MUSIC 2014 (SECTION C)

SAMPLE QUESTION 1

Compare and contrast the approach to resources and texture in the three pieces listed below. (36)

➢   Beethoven – Septet in E♭ major, Op. 20: movement I

➢   Schumann – *Kinderscenen* Nos. 1, 3 and 11

➢   Debussy – *Pour le piano*: Sarabande

Before studying the mark scheme (indicative content) that follows, attempt the question yourself. Notice that the key words are *resources* and *texture*. You may find it convenient to refer briefly to the context of each work, but take care to keep your remarks relevant. Do not waste time on any aspects of the works that do not concern texture or resources.

Indicative content	
Resources	**Beethoven** Typical Classical 'serenade' band: three wind, four strings including double bass for extra weight. **Schumann** Piano, central range mainly used. **Debussy** Piano, full range used with constant use of the sustaining pedal.
Texture	**Beethoven** • Mainly homophonic • Chords for varying numbers of parts • Monophony • Antiphonal exchange/dialogue • Melody-dominated homophony • Some broken-chord accompaniment • Some syncopated inner parts • Octaves • Thematic combination. **Schumann** • No. 1: in three parts (mainly), melody-and-accompaniment with broken chords in the middle; detached quavers in the bass masked by the sustaining pedal; 3rds in RH at bar 9 in counterpoint with the bass

- No. 3: leaping/'stride' LH with mainly single-line melody; more sustained writing from bar 13 leading to a longer chord at bar 15, with an ascending scale in the middle part

- No. 11: three-part texture, broadening to four parts; bass melody with off-beat RH chords; chords for all parts.

Debussy

- Mainly homophonic

- Varying densities and registers

- Octaves

- Melody with independent chordal accompaniment

- Parallel 4th, 6th and 7th chords.

Sample answer 1

The works are dealt with in chronological order. Beethoven disliked the Septet, apparently, because it seemed to him to be too Classical. It is an outstanding example of this style, having the sort of instrumental line-up (with double bass) that makes it suitable for outdoor performance as a serenade or divertimento [1]. It is fundamentally homophonic in texture throughout [1]. Having said that, Beethoven obtained considerable variety within the work, partly by varying the number of players performing at any one time, and also by changing the type of texture used:

> Bar 1 – tutti chords [1 – **located**]
> Bar 2 – monophonic violin [1 – **located**]
> Bar 8 – chords in three parts for strings [1 – **located**]
> Bar 19 – melody-dominated homophony [1 – **located**] with broken-chord figure in viola
> Bar 29 – tutti mdh, with syncopated inner parts [1 – **located**]
> Bar 40 – monophonic solo violin
> Bar 47 – antiphonal exchange between wind instruments, answered by strings [1 – **located**]
> Bar 86 – three-part string chords
> Bar 111 – mainly octaves [1 – **located**].

Schumann only had a piano for his piece, so the range of textures won't be so large:

> No. 1: three-part mdh, with broken chord in middle part [1]

Avoid underlining in continuous prose.

Avoid abbreviations in continuous prose.

This type of texture has already been credited.

This has already been credited.

> ➤ No. 3: oom-pah LH [1]   ◄──────────────────────── | Accept. |
> ➤ No. 11: mdh, but here the LH has the tune sometimes
>   (bar 9) [1].

Debussy was also writing for a single piano, but had a much wider range of sounds and timbres because of the range available [1] and he also used the sustaining pedal frequently [1]. He varied textures constantly:

> ➤ Bar 1: six-part homophony (block chords)
>   [1 – located]
> ➤ Bar 9: independent melody and chordal
>   accompaniment [1 – located]
> ➤ Bar 23: parallel 4th chords [1 – located]
> ➤ Etc.

Examiner's points

17 points were made, with some illustrated. Unfortunately, the mark will have to be adjusted because of the bullet-list format, use of underlinings and abbreviations, none of which should really appear in a passage of continuous prose. A mark of **22/36** is appropriate.

Exercise

Rewrite the paragraph on Schumann in continuous prose, expanding on the points already made.

Sample answer 2

Mark this answer yourself, commenting at the end on its good points, but also mentioning ways in which it could have been improved. After completing your marking, check your assessment against the examiner's points below.

The most varied textures are to be found in the Beethoven. This is scarcely surprising as the other two pieces are for piano. Admittedly Debussy made full use of the instrument, both with regard to the wide range exploited and the use of the sustaining pedal, which permitted the creation of some impressive sonorities. Although fundamentally homophonic, Debussy varied the densities and registers throughout to maintain interest. He starts with six-part chords, moves on to octaves at bar 5, then on to a rhythmically independent melody with chordal accompaniment at bar 9. The first section ends at bars 20–21 with low octaves. In the middle section, Debussy uses different harmonies and sonorities, namely parallel 4ths and then streams of parallel 6ths (bar 35).

Working backwards chronologically, the Schumann uses melody-dominated homophony throughout. In the case of the first piece, he writes a typically Romantic texture, with the melody in the top part, accompanied by triplet broken chords in the middle and supported by quavers in the bass, sustained by way of the pedal. At one point the top part is doubled in 3rds, and is heard in a sort of counterpoint with the bass.

The second piece has a stride bass accompaniment, with the low bass alternating with a higher chord. The most varied textures come in the final piece, which opens with a melody line in the right hand with a rhythmically independent accompaniment in the left hand. At bar 5, Schumann reverses the roles, with the previous melody placed in the left hand. He carries on with this method at bar 9, but here the melody is accompanied with off-beat right-hand chords. Very briefly, Schumann also uses block chords (bar 24).

Beethoven's Septet opens with a chord for all seven instruments, answered by monophonic violin. The introduction also uses homophony for three instruments, and latterly the violin is given a rhythmically independent melody line. The first subject of the sonata-form proper is given to three instruments in a melody-dominated homophonic texture. The melody is given to the violin, supported by the viola with broken chords and the cello providing intermittent crotchets. When this theme is repeated at bar 29, the clarinet takes the melody, supported by sustained notes on the other wind instruments and syncopations in the upper strings, and a steady crotchet figure in the cello. Another textural device is a form of antiphony or dialogue between the wind and strings at bar 47, and Beethoven also uses most of the instruments in octaves at the start of the development.

Of the three works, Beethoven's is the most interesting. He achieves more contrast than can be found in the other works, partly by varying the number of instruments in play as well as changing the textural layout rapidly.

Examiner's points

Credit can be awarded for:

Debussy:

➢ Full use of piano range

➢ Use of sustaining pedal

➢ Six-part chords (located)

➢ Octaves (located)

➢ Rhythmically independent melody and chordal accompaniment (located)

➢ Very low octaves (located)

➢ Parallel 4ths (not precisely located)

➢ Parallel 6ths (located).

Schumann:

➢ Melody-dominated homophony

➢ Implied three parts in No. 1

➢ Broken-chord middle part

➢ Quaver bass part

➢ Upper part in 3rds with bass counterpoint (not located)

➢ Stride bass

➢ Reversal of left- and right-hand roles (located)

➢ Off-beat chords (located)

➢ Block chords (located).

Beethoven:

➢ Tutti opening chord (located)

➢ Monophonic line (located)

➢ Three-part chords (not precisely located)

➢ Description of texture at bar 19 (not located)

➢ Description of texture at bar 29 (located)

➢ Antiphonal exchange (located)

➢ Octaves (located).

There were 24 valid points, many well-illustrated. The essay was well-written and had some sort of plan in that it worked backwards chronologically, keeping the Beethoven to the end. More could have been said about the resources Beethoven used, but this work would be placed in the top category with **32/36**.

Exercise

Insert a couple of sentences at the start of the fourth paragraph, describing the resources Beethoven employed.

SAMPLE QUESTION 2

Compare and contrast the use of harmony and tonality in the three pieces listed below. (36)

➢ **J. S. Bach – Brandenburg Concerto No. 4 in G: movement I**

➢ **Sweelinck – *Pavana Lachrimae***

➢ **Duke Ellington and his Orchestra – *Black and Tan Fantasy***

Before studying the mark scheme (indicative content) that follows, attempt the question yourself. Notice that the key words are *harmony* and *tonality*. You may find it convenient to refer briefly to the context of each work, but take care to keep your remarks relevant. Points should be illustrated with examples from the music.

Indicative content	
Harmony	**Bach**
	• Functional
	• Mainly diatonic
	• Cadences
	• Chords in root position and all inversions
	• Dominant 7ths
	• Neapolitan 6th when the music moves to a minor key
	• Frequent harmonic sequences
	• Circle of 5ths
	• Pedal points
	• Suspensions.

	Sweelinck • Mainly root-position and first-inversion chords • Phrygian cadences • Perfect cadences • 4–3 and 7–6 suspensions. **Ellington** • Based on 12-bar blues • Substitution chords • Circle of 5ths • Plagal cadence at end.
Tonality	**Bach** • Modulations to related keys. **Sweelinck** • A minor with Aeolian-mode inflections • Dominant pedal • Tierce de Picardie • Short passage in relative major • Occasional false relations. **Ellington** • Opens in B♭ minor • Central passage in B♭ major (at bar 13) • Ends in B♭ minor (at bar 87).

Sample answer 1

The works will be dealt with in chronological order to show how approaches to harmony and tonality have progressed over time. Sweelinck and Bach are both Baroque composers, and it is not surprising to find that over the 100 years that separated the composition of their works chord choice became much more sophisticated. They both used cadences. In Sweelinck it was mainly perfect [1] and Phrygian [1] cadences, i.e. IVb–V in a minor key.

In the Sweelinck chord choice was relatively limited, and this was mainly because of the primitive tonal system he used.

> Perhaps the candidate did not mean it, but the implication is that earlier music is somehow not as advanced as that of more recent times!

> At this level it is not necessary to spell out chord progressions in cadences.

> Limited to what chords?

He still had to escape the feeling of modality, and there are plenty of traces of the Aeolian mode [1]. The signs of this are evident in the false relations that crop up from time to time, e.g. the clash of G♮ and G♯ in bar 10 [1 – **illustrated point**]. Another sign of old-fashioned writing is the use of a tierce de Picardie [1] at the end of all the main sections, although interestingly the middle ones come on chords of E major, showing some attempt at modulation. ◄

> The candidate has mistakenly assumed that the major chord here was automatically a tierce de Picardie, whereas it is the final chord of a Phrygian cadence.

With Bach, we have a work that uses functional harmonies [1], and this makes for a much more complex structure. Sweelinck's piece is simply in three unconnected sections: AA'BB'CC', which is not very sophisticated, whereas Bach uses a lengthy ritornello form with many modulations [1] to all manner of keys. An extended and complicated form like this would not have been possible without the variety that comes with different keys.

As noted above, Bach relies on cadences to mark important points in the progress of the music. Other 'functional' features include a circle of 5ths [1], and sequences in general [1]. He also uses pedal points [1]. Choice of chords is not perhaps as wide-ranging as in other works by Bach, but when the music goes into a minor key, he sometimes introduces a Neapolitan 6th chord [1].

To return to tonality, the range of keys modulated to in the Bach is wide and includes dominant, subdominant, relative minor, and relative minors of the subdominant and dominant [1]. ◄

> It is only possible to award one mark for this sentence as the candidate has really only stated that the modulations are to related keys. Marks would be awarded for specific keys only if substantiating locations were offered.

One would expect that with the passing of time approaches to tonality would get more complex, but *Black and Tan Fantasy*, though more involved harmonically than either the Sweelinck or Bach works, is certainly less enterprising than Bach in terms of tonality. ◄

> An effective linking contrast.

It starts in B♭ minor [1 – **illustrated point**], the largest part in the middle starting at bar 13 is in the tonic major [1 – **illustrated point**], and the music returns to B♭ minor for the final four bars [1 – **illustrated point**].

The harmony is initially dictated by the 12-bar blues pattern [1], but as the piece unfolds, Ellington uses some unusual additional harmonies, for example the G♭⁷ at bar 13, which working as a German 6th leads onto the tonic B♭ major at bar 15 [1 – **illustrated point**]. ◄

> The mark is not for reading off the chord indication, but describing its function.

Other noteworthy features include the diminished 7th [1], the circle of 5ths [1], and the final string of plagal cadences [1 – **location given**].

Examiner's points

The candidate made 20 points, but generally offered little substantiation. There was some irrelevance as well as an unfortunate basic view of the nature of music history. The answer would be awarded a mark of **24/36**.

Exercise

Remove or modify the more opinionated sections, and provide bar references where needed.

Sample answer 2

Mark this answer yourself, commenting at the end on its good points, but also mentioning ways in which it could have been improved. After completing your marking, check your assessment against the examiner's points below.

> Bach's concerto is in G. Sweelinck's *Pavana Lachrimae* is in A minor. Ellington's piece is also in a minor key (B♭ minor). All three pieces also have passages in major keys.
> Ellington uses substitution chords. The harmonies at the start are easy to see: B♭m, E♭m, B♭m, F⁷, B♭m, E♭m, B♭m, G♭⁷, B♭, E♭⁷, B♭, C⁷, F⁷, then nothing happens for the rest of the page.
> Bach doesn't use substitution chords, but he does use dominant 7ths. Sweelink modulates to C major at bar 33. Ellington finishes with a plagal cadence. Bach doesn't use plagal cadences, but he finishes with a perfect cadence.
> Bach uses remote keys like B minor.
> Ellington uses substitute chords. Unlike Ellington, Sweelinck finishes on a major chord. Bach often uses a tonic pedal. Ellington's piece is a sort of variation piece built on the 12-bar blues.
> Bach uses a circle of 5ths at bars 119–125. So does Ellington. Sweelinck doesn't.
> Ellington uses pitch bends to vary the harmonies. Sweelinck also uses a dominant pedal.

Examiner's points

Marks can be awarded here for:

➢ Naming the keys of *Pavana Lachrimae* and *Black and Tan Fantasy* (not the Brandenburg Concerto, as the key appears in the title)

➢ Use of substitution chords in *Black and Tan Fantasy*

➢ Dominant 7ths in Bach

➢   Modulation to C at bar 33 in the *Pavana* (location given)

➢   Plagal cadence at the end of *Black and Tan Fantasy* (location given)

➢   Perfect cadence at the end of the Bach (location given)

➢   Tonic pedal in the Bach

➢   12-bar blues in the Ellington

➢   Circle of 5ths in the Bach (location given)

➢   Dominant pedal in the Sweelinck.

Notice that credit was not awarded for key references that were not located precisely; reading off the chord descriptions from the score of *Black and Tan Fantasy*; and negative statements.

There was no evidence of planning, the whole piece being little more than a random stringing together of facts, not all of which were fully illustrated.

As there were 11 points with limited illustration, and weak organisation, this piece would be awarded **17/36**.

Exercise

Organise the answer above, grouping points together logically and providing bar references where appropriate.

Glossary

This glossary is not comprehensive: it refers to terms as used in this volume. For more information about harmonic terms (e.g. suspension) see the AS Harmony Workbook *and/or the* A2 Harmony Workbook *by Hugh Benham (Rhinegold, 2008). For fuller definitions of other terms and expressions consult the* Dictionary of Music in Sound *by David Bowman (Rhinegold, 2002).*

Acciaccatura. A very short ornamental note played before a principal melodic note, written or printed as ♪.

Additive rhythm. Where a bar has beats of unequal length, or where unequal short rhythmic sets are grouped together to form a longer rhythmic pattern.

Aeolian mode. A scale that uses the following pattern of tones (T) and semitones (s): T–s–T–T–s–T–T. When starting on A, it consists of all the white notes within one octave on a keyboard.

Alberti bass. A particular type of broken-chord pattern often found in classical keyboard music with three pitches heard in the order low-high-middle-high, e.g. C–G–E–G.

Anacrusis. Note or notes preceding the first beat of a piece or phrase.

Angular. When applied to melody, the presence of wide leaps.

Anthem. A type of church music for choir, often accompanied by organ, and occasionally by larger forces. An anthem usually has English words (often from the Bible).

Antiphony. Performance by different singers/instrumentalists in alternation. Often – but not always – the different groups perform similar material.

Appoggiatura. A non-chord note that sounds on the beat as a dissonance and then resolves by step (up or down) to the main chord note. The dissonant note is not 'prepared' as a suspension is. Although appoggiaturas are normally approached by leap, accented passing notes that are particularly long and/or prominent are often described as appoggiaturas, even though they are approached by step. Sometimes an appoggiatura, especially in the Classical period, is indicated by a note in small type, followed by its resolution printed at normal size.

Arco. A direction to bow notes on a string instrument.

Aria. A song (usually from an **opera**, oratorio or **cantata**) for solo voice, plus accompaniment for orchestra or, sometimes in Baroque times, for smaller forces, even just **continuo**. An aria often provides a character in an opera with the opportunity to reflect at length on their emotional state.

Articulation. The manner in which a series of notes are played with regards to their separation or connection – for example, staccato (separated) or legato (connected).

Atonal. Atonal music avoids keys or modes; that is, no pitch stands out consistently in the way that the tonic does in tonal music.

Augmentation. The lengthening of the rhythmic values of a previously-heard melody (e.g. where ♩ ♫ has become ♩ ♩ ♩).

Augmented triad. A three-note chord in which the interval between successive notes is a major 3rd; for example, the chord D–F♯–A♯.

Augmented 6th chord. A chromatic chord which in root position spans the interval of an augmented 6th, e.g. A♭–F♯.

Bebop. A style of jazz that developed in the 1940s from swing. More complex and less easy to dance to, it was characterised by **improvisation**, fast tempos, irregular phrase lengths and a greater emphasis on the rhythm section.

Binary form. A structure consisting of two sections, the first of which closes in a related key and the second in the tonic. This structure was frequently used by Baroque composers, e.g. in dance movements.

Bitonal. Music that uses two different keys simultaneously.

Broken chord. The performing of the notes of a chord one after another instead of simultaneously.

Cadence. A pair of chords signifying the end of a phrase in tonal music. Cadences are of several types, of which perfect and imperfect are by far the most common. *See also* **Imperfect cadence, Interrupted cadence, Perfect cadence, Plagal cadence** and **Phrygian cadence**.

Cadential 6–4. Chord Ic, preceding chord V or V^7 in a perfect or imperfect cadence.

Calypso. A genre of song from Trinidad characterised by humorous or subversive lyrics. The music itself merges European and African elements.

Cambiata. Generally used to describe the movement from an unaccented non-harmony note which is quitted by a leap of a 3rd.

Canon. A strict form of **imitation**, in which each successive part repeats exactly the music of the first part.

Cantata. Most commonly a work for voice(s) and instruments in several movements, with **aria**(s), **recitative**(s) and chorus(es). A cantata can be sacred or secular.

Cantus firmus. An already existing melody (frequently plainchant or a **chorale**) to which other freely composed parts are added to make a new piece.

Chorale. A German hymn of the kind sung in the Lutheran (Protestant) church in the time of J. S. Bach. The word 'chorale' can refer to the words only, to the associated melody only, or to the whole hymn. Chorale melodies are largely stepwise (or **conjunct**); their harmonisation has long featured in advanced music courses.

Chordal. A form of homophony in which all the parts move together in the same or very similar rhythm. The term **homorhythmic** (literally 'same rhythm') is sometimes used instead.

Chromatic. A chromatic note is one that does not belong to the scale of the key currently in use. For example, in D major the notes G♯ and C♮ are chromatic. Music that is chromatic contains many chromatic notes.

Circle of 5ths. A harmonic progression in which the roots of the chords move by descending 5ths (and/or ascending 4ths), e.g. B–E–A–D–G–C etc.

Coda. A concluding section of a movement.

Comping. A term associated with jazz and popular music referring to the playing of a **chordal** accompaniment.

Compound time. A metre in which the main beat is subdivided into three equal portions, as opposed to two equal portions in **simple time**.

Concerto. Most commonly, a work for a soloist with orchestra. In many concertos the solo instrument is a piano or violin. Occasionally there may be two soloists (a double concerto) or even three (a triple concerto). (In the 17th century the term was used more widely, and was applied originally to a work in which voices and instruments, with more or less independent parts, collaborated in a manner that was new at the time.) *See also* **Concerto grosso**.

Concerto grosso. A type of concerto, most common in the late Baroque period, in which three (or occasionally more) soloists, known as the 'concertino', are contrasted with the sound of a larger group of mainly string instruments, know as the 'ripieno'.

Conjunct. Melodic movement by step rather than by leap. Opposite of **disjunct**.

Continuo. Short for 'basso continuo', the continuo instruments form the accompaniment in Baroque music. It may include instruments such as the harpsichord (capable of playing full harmony) and a cello or bassoon reinforcing the bass line.

Contrapuntal. Adjective to describe music that uses **counterpoint**.

Counterpoint. Counterpoint involves two or more melodic lines (usually rhythmically contrasted), each significant in itself, which are played or sung together at the same time. The term polyphonic is often used as a synonym for contrapuntal.

Counter-subject. In a fugue, the melodic material that is heard in counterpoint with the answer.

Cross rhythm. The use of two or more very different rhythms simultaneously in different parts. One rhythm may imply one metre (or time signature), while another implies a different one.

Development. The central part of a **sonata form** movement between the **exposition** and the recapitulation, containing a working-out of ideas already heard in the exposition.

Dialogue. When two or more instruments or voices have a musical 'conversation', with the individual parts responding to one another.

Diatonic. Using notes that belong to the current key. A diatonic note is one that belongs to the scale of the key currently in use. For example, in D major the notes D, E and F♯ are diatonic.

Diminished 7th chord. A four-note chord made up of superimposed minor 3rds.

Diminished interval. An interval that is one semitone narrower than a minor or perfect interval. A diminished 4th (e.g. G♯–C) is one semitone narrower than a perfect 4th (G–

C); a diminished 6th (e.g. B–G♭) is one semitone narrower than a minor 6th (B–G).

Diminution. The shortening of the rhythmic values of a previously-heard melody (e.g. where ♩ ♩ ♩ has become ♩ ♫).

Disjunct. Melodic movement by leap rather than by step. Opposite of **conjunct**.

Dissonance. Strictly speaking, any note not belonging to a triad in root position or first inversion (even the 4th above the bass in a second inversion counts as dissonant). Some dissonances, particularly suspensions and appoggiaturas, add tension, which in early music had to be 'resolved'; others, notably passing and auxiliary notes, provide rhythmic and melodic decoration.

Divertimento. A piece (most commonly from the 18th century) whose style is partly or wholly light and intended to 'divert' or 'amuse' listeners, perhaps at a social function. A divertimento is normally in several movements, with at least one in a dance (particularly minuet) style.

Dominant 7th chord. A four-note chord built on the dominant (fifth) note of the scale. It includes the dominant triad plus a minor 7th above the root.

Dorian mode. A scale that uses the following pattern of tones (T) and semitones (s): T–s–T–T–T–s–T. When starting on D, it consists of all the white notes within one octave on a keyboard.

Double-stopping. The playing of two notes simultaneously on adjacent strings of a string instrument. The term is sometimes used loosely to cover three- and four-note multiple stopping. *See also* **Triple-stopping**.

Drone. A sustained note (or notes frequently forming an interval of a 5th) held in one part while other parts play or sing melodies against it.

Dynamics. How loudly or softly the music is played; the volume of the music. Indicated by dynamic markings such as *piano* (quiet) and *crescendo* (gradually get louder).

Exposition. The first section of a **sonata form** movement, typically including the first subject in the tonic and the second subject in a related key.

Fall off. In jazz, a short downward slide ending in silence.

False relation. The occurrence of the ordinary and chromatically altered versions of the same note (such as F♮ and F♯) in two different parts at the same time, or in close proximity.

Figured bass. A figured bass is an instrumental bass part with 'figures' or 'figuring' (chiefly numerals and sharp, flat and natural signs) designed to show a continuo keyboard or lute player what type of chord to play.

First inversion. *See* **Inversion**.

Fortspinnung. The spinning out of a melody line typically by repetition, sequence, variation of intervals, inversion, etc. The term is frequently applied in analysis of Baroque music.

Fractal scheme. A term sometimes used to describe Cage's 'micro-macrocosmic' structures: a self-symmetrical scheme in which each segment is a miniature version of the whole.

Fragmentation. The splitting up of melodic lines into shorter components, which are then treated in isolation.

Fugal. *See* **Fugue**.

Fugato. A passage in **fugal** style which forms part of a larger of music.

Fugue. A type of piece in which a main theme called a 'subject' is treated in imitation by all the parts. 'Episodes' are the contrasting sections which depart from this pattern.

Functional harmony. A type of harmony that gravitates to the tonic through use of a hierarchy of chords, the dominant being second only to the tonic, and cadences.

Galliard. A fast triple-time dance of the Renaissance era, usually consisting of three repeated sections (A A, B B, C C). It was frequently paired with a **pavan(e)**.

Gamelan. An ensemble from Indonesia (usually Bali or Java) consisting largely of tuned percussion.

Ghost note. In jazz, a note that is deliberately played so faintly as to be almost inaudible.

Gigue. A quick, lively Baroque dance commonly in compound time, it was one of the key components of a Baroque (dance) suite.

Glissando. A slide from one pitch to another.

Gongan. In **gamelan** music, a rhythmic unit concluded by the sounding of the gong.

Half-valving. The partial opening of a valve on a brass instrument to result in a weak tone and unfocused pitch. The technique is particularly used in jazz.

Harmonics. A technique of lightly touching the string (e.g. on a violin) to produce a high, flute-like sound.

Head. In jazz and popular music, the basic substance of the number which is then varied. The structure is sometimes referred to as a head arrangement.

Hemiola. The articulation of two units of triple time (strong–weak–weak, strong–weak–weak) as three units of duple time (strong–weak, strong–weak, strong–weak).

Heterophony. A type of texture in which a melody is performed simultaneously with one or more rhythmically and/or melodically varied versions of itself.

Homophony. A texture in which one part has a melody and the other parts accompany, in contrast to contrapuntal writing, where each part has independent melodic and rhythmic interest.

Homorhythm. *See* **Chordal**.

Idée fixe. A term associated originally with Berlioz's music, signifying a recurring musical **motif**.

Imitation. Where a melodic idea in one part is immediately repeated in another part (exactly or inexactly), at the same or a different pitch, while the first part continues. Described with the adjective imitative.

Imperfect cadence. An open-ended cadence in which the dominant chord (V) is preceded by any other suitable chord, often I, ii or IV.

Impressionism. A compositional movement that began in France in the late 19th century and continued into the 20th, and was in some respects similar to the art movement of the same name. Important characteristics of impressionist music include heightened attention to timbre, colour and atmosphere, non-functional harmony and tonality and fluid metre.

Improvisation. Characteristic of jazz, the spontaneous creation of new music, often based on existing musical material (such as a chord pattern).

Incidental music. Music usually written for stage, film or television, which establishes an appropriate atmosphere for the action it accompanies.

Interrupted cadence. A cadence most frequently consisting of chords V–VI, designed to defeat expectations by avoiding chord I.

Inversion (harmonic). When a chord has a note other than the root in the lowest part, it is an inversion. In a first-inversion chord the 3rd of the chord is in the lowest part, and in a second-inversion chord the 5th. For example, a triad of F major in first inversion is A–C–F, and in second inversion is C–F–A. *See also* **Root position**.

Inversion (melodic). When a melody line is heard upside down, e.g. pitches C–E–D are presented as C–A–B.

Inverted pedal. A pedal note which is held in a higher part of the texture, rather than in the bass.

Ionian mode. A scale that uses the following pattern of tones (T) and semitones (s): T–T–s–T–T–T–s. When starting on C, it consists of all the white notes within one octave on a keyboard.

Keteg. In **gamelan** music, individual rhythmic cells, the equivalent of bars, which together form the gongan.

Klangfarbenmelodie. German for 'sound-colour-melody'. A musical technique in which a melodic line is distributed among more than one instrument, thereby producing different timbres depending on which instruments are used.

Leading note. The seventh degree of a major or minor scale, usually with a strong tendency to rise to the tonic.

Leitmotif. A theme that is associated with a character, situation, mood, object or idea, especially in the operas of Richard Wagner and dramatic works/film music of later composers.

Libretto. The script or words for a dramatic work that is set to music (e.g. an opera, musical or oratorio).

Lydian mode. A scale that uses the following pattern of tones (T) and semitones (s): T–T–T–s–T–T–s. When starting on F, it consists of all the white notes within one octave on a keyboard. When the fourth is raised in a major scale, this is sometimes termed a Lydian inflection.

Melismatic. The setting of several notes to one syllable.

Melody-dominated homophony. A melody and accompaniment texture in which the accompaniment is not strictly chordal.

Metre. The metre refers to the pulse of the music and is indicated by the time signature.

Miniature. A short instrumental piece that depicts a scene or represents a mood.

Minimalism. A 20th- and 21st-century often deliberately simple style of composing based on repetitions of short melodic and rhythmic patterns. It was developed by American composers such as Steve Reich, Philip Glass and Terry Riley.

Modal. A term often used to refer to music based on a mode rather than on major and minor keys.

Modulation. A change of key, or the process of changing key.

Monody. A term used in connection with early Baroque music in particular, referring to a solo vocal line accompanied by continuo instruments only.

Monophony. Music consisting only of a single melodic line. Also described with the adjective 'monophonic'.

Motet. A type of church music for choir, sometimes accompanied by organ, and occasionally by larger forces. A motet often has Latin words (commonly from the Bible), and is particularly but not exclusively associated with Roman Catholic services. Motets were often composed for specific occasions, unlike the Ordinary of the Mass.

Motif. A short but distinctive musical idea that is developed in various ways in order to create a longer passage of music. The adjective is 'motivic'.

Neapolitan 6th chord. A chromatic chord (often in a minor key) consisting of the first inversion of the major chord formed on the flattened supertonic, i.e. the second degree of the scale (in D minor, for example, the Neapolitan 6th has the notes G–B♭–E♭).

Neoclassical. In music the adjective 'neoclassical' is most widely applied to certain early and mid 20th-century styles that combine a clear debt to previous eras (notably the Baroque and the Classical) with more up-to-date elements.

Obbligato. A prominent (and essential – 'obligatory') instrumental part in Baroque music, often in an aria, in addition to the vocal part and **continuo**.

Opera. A large-scale dramatic work for singers and instrumentalists in which the whole text is sung.

Ornamentation. Addition of melodic decoration, often through the use of conventional forms such as trills and mordents.

Ostinato. A repeating melodic, harmonic or rhythmic motif, heard continuously throughout part or the whole of a piece.

Parallelism. Also known as parallel harmony, this is the parallel movement of two or more melodic lines or chords.

Passing note. A non-harmony note approached and quitted by step in the same direction, often filling in a melodic gap of a 3rd (e.g. A between G and B, where both G and B are harmony notes).

Pavan(e). Slow, quadruple-time dance of the Renaissance era, usually consisting of three repeated sections (A A, B B, C C).

Pedal (note). A sustained or repeated note, usually in a low register, over which changing harmonies occur. A pedal on the fifth note of the scale (a dominant pedal) tends to create a sense of expectation in advance of a perfect cadence; a pedal on the keynote (a tonic pedal) can create a feeling of repose.

Pelog. In gamelan music, a seven-note scale. Often, only five notes from such a scale are actually used.

Pentatonic. A scale made up of five notes, most frequently the first, second, third, fifth and sixth degrees of a major scale (for example, C pentatonic is C–D–E–G–A).

Perfect cadence. A cadence consisting of the dominant chord (V or V[7]) followed by the tonic (I).

Periodic phrasing. In Classical-period music particularly, where phrases of regular length are heard in balanced structures.

The expression 'antecedent and consequent' is sometimes applied to these phrases.

Phrygian cadence. A type of imperfect cadence, in which the dominant chord (V) is preceded by the first inversion of the subdominant (IVb). It is used chiefly in minor keys, and particularly in Baroque music.

Pitch bend. In jazz, a microtonal variation in pitch.

Pizzicato (often abbreviated to **pizz.**). A direction to pluck, instead of bow, string(s) on a violin, viola, cello or double bass. Cancelled by the direction '**arco**' – with the bow.

Plagal cadence. A cadence consisting of the subdominant chord followed by the tonic (IV–I).

Pointillism. Originally referring to a painting technique, in which small dots of colour are carefully placed to create a larger image, this refers to a musical effect in which different notes are played or sung in isolation from each other, rather than as part of a musical line, thereby sketching out a larger musical form.

Polyphony. Sometimes used as an alternative term for **counterpoint**, especially in relation to Renaissance music.

Polyrhythm. The use of more than one rhythm at the same time, often implying the presence of different metres.

Post-modernism. A style of composition that deliberately contrasts itself with modernist concepts, and the highly intellectual approach (typified by serialism) associated with them. Post-modernism tries to avoid categorising music rigidly, and often incorporates fragments of works and references to other cultures in a more approachable style.

Prime order. In **serialism**, the original order in which the notes of a tone-row are played.

Programmatic. Music with a stimulus that comes from outside the music itself.

Quartal harmony. Harmony based on the interval of a 4th (e.g. with chords such as A–D–G), rather than on the interval of a 3rd as in triads and 7th chords.

Quarter tone. Half a semitone.

Recapitulation. In **sonata form**, the section which follows the **development**. It is often closely based on the **exposition**, but normally both opens and closes in the tonic key.

Recitative. A piece for solo voice in an **opera, cantata** or oratorio (often before an **aria**) in which clear projection of words is the main concern. In many recitatives the music is functional rather than of great interest in itself, with the accompaniment often just for **continuo**.

Retrograde. The pitches of a previously heard melody or rhythm presented in reverse order.

Riff. In popular music styles, a short repeating phrase.

Ritornello form. A structure used in Baroque music in which an opening instrumental section (called the ritornello) introduces the main musical ideas. This returns, often in shortened versions and in related keys, between passages for one or more soloists. The complete ritornello (or a substantial part of it) returns in the tonic key at the end.

Rondo. A form in which the main theme (or subject) returns periodically in the tonic key. Simple rondo takes the form A–B–A–C–A etc., while Sonata rondo involves recapitulation of a second subject as well as the first: A–B(related key)–A–C(development)–A–B(tonic)–A. This form came to be used frequently in finales.

Root position. A chord that has the root in the lowest sounding part.

Rounded binary form. A variation of simple **binary form** (AB), in which a thematic reference to the beginning of the moment is made at the end of the B section.

Rubato. The variation of pulse by subtle lengthening and shortening of notes, so producing a free rhythmic feel.

Saltarello. A lively dance in $\frac{6}{8}$ which originated from Naples in the 13th century.

Scherzo. A fast movement which eventually replaced the minuet of the Classical era.

Secondary dominant. A passing or temporary dominant hinting at a different key, e.g. in C major, an E major chord acting as dominant to a tonic of A minor.

Secondary 7th. A 7th chord built on a degree of the scale other than the dominant.

Second inversion. See **Inversion**.

Sequence. Immediate repetition of a melodic or harmonic idea at a different pitch.

Serial. In serial music all (or most) pitches are derived from an underlying fixed series of pitches that can be manipulated by transposition, inversion and retrograding (being played backwards). A widely practised form of serialism in the mid 20th century used a series (or 'row') of twelve notes that included every note of the chromatic scale once.

Simple time. A metre in which the main beat is sub-divided into two equal portions. Opposite of **compound time**.

Sonata. An instrumental work, commonly in three or four movements. From the late Baroque period onwards, sonatas are usually for solo keyboard or for single melody instrument and keyboard. 'Trio sonatas' (middle to late Baroque) are normally for two violins and continuo.

Sonata form. Typical first movement form of the Classical and Romantic periods. In three sections – **exposition, development, recapitulation** – often based on two groups of melodic material in two contrasting keys (first subject, second subject).

Stretto. The overlapping of imitative entries more closely than had previously occurred, used especially in connection with **fugal** writing.

Stride. A jazz piano style partly derived from ragtime, in particular from the characteristic left-hand pattern which repeatedly 'strides' from a low note or chord on a strong beat to an often much higher chord on a weak beat. Stride piano was especially popular in the 1920s.

Substitution chord. A chord that is substituted for another chord for the sake of variety. In particular the term is used in jazz.

Suspension. A suspension occurs at a change of chord, when one part hangs on to (or repeats) a note from the old chord, creating a clash, after which the delayed part resolves by step (usually down) to a note of the new chord.

Swung rhythm. In jazz and other popular music, a certain freedom in performance whereby rhythms that might in other contexts be played 'straight' as equal notes are performed with the first of each pair longer than the second, often giving a kind of triplet effect.

Syllabic. The setting of one note to one syllable.

Symphony. A work for orchestra with several (usually three or four) movements in different tempi – in effect a sonata for orchestra rather than for one or a few instruments.

Syncopation. The shifting of stress from a strong to a weak beat. For example, in a $\frac{4}{4}$

bar with the rhythm ♩ ♩ ♩, the minim (a relatively long note beginning on a weak beat) is syncopated.

Ternary form. A musical structure of three sections in which the outer sections are similar and the central one contrasting (ABA).

Tertiary progression.   When roots of chords or key areas proceed by 3rds.

Tessitura. A specific part of a singer's or instrument's range. For example a 'high tessitura' indicates a high part of the range.

Texture. The relationship between the various simultaneous lines in a passage of music, dependent on such features as the number and function of the parts and the spacing between them.

Through-composed. Applied to music in which the composer avoids repetition of previous material, i.e. fresh material for different phrases in a vocal work.

Tierce de Picardie. A major 3rd in the final tonic chord of a passage in a minor key.

Timbre. The element of music concerned with the actual sound quality, or tone colour, of the music.

Tonality. Music is described as being tonal when one note is of central importance, other notes being subordinate. The note of central importance is termed the tonic when major and minor keys and scales are used. In 18th-and 19th-century music tonality is established and maintained by **functional harmony**, but tonality can be based instead on other types of scales, notably **modes**.

Transition. A linking passage.

Tremolo. A rapid and continuous repetition of a single note or two alternating notes.

Trill. An ornament in which two adjacent notes rapidly and repeatedly alternate (the note bearing the trill sign and the one above it). The symbol for trill is *tr*.

Trio sonata. A musical form prevalent in the Baroque era, a trio sonata is written for two solo melody instruments and basso continuo, making three parts in total (hence the name 'trio' sonata); however, the continuo part would normally have had two or more instruments playing, usually a cello or bass viol and a harpsichord.

Triple-stopping. The playing of three notes simultaneously (or as near simultaneously as possible) on adjacent strings of a string instrument. *See also* **Double-stopping.**

Triplet. A group of three equal notes played in the time normally taken by two notes of the same type.

Tritone. An interval that is equivalent to three tones (an augmented 4th or dimished 5th).

Turn. A four-note ornament that 'turns' around the main note. It starts on the note above, drops to the main note, drops to the note below and then returns to the main note. Indicated by the symbol ∾.

Twelve-bar blues. A standard chord sequence used in the blues and other popular music, which is based on the tonic (I), subdominant (IV) and dominant (V) chords of a key. Its most common form is I–I–I–I, IV–IV–I–I, V–IV–I–I.

Unison. Simultaneous performance of the same note or melody by two or more players or singers.

Walking bass. A bass part that persistently uses the same note length.

Whole-tone scale. A scale in which the interval between every successive note is a whole tone.